Knights Templar

The True And Surprising Story Of Histories Most Secretive Order

(The Hidden History Of The Knights Templar)

Steven Price

Published By **Bella Frost**

Steven Price

All Rights Reserved

Knights Templar: The True And Surprising Story Of Histories Most Secretive Order (The Hidden History Of The Knights Templar)

ISBN 978-1-77485-593-5

No part of this guidebook shall be reproduced in any form without permission in writing from the publisher except in the case of brief quotations embodied in critical articles or reviews.

Legal & Disclaimer

The information contained in this ebook is not designed to replace or take the place of any form of medicine or professional medical advice. The information in this ebook has been provided for educational & entertainment purposes only.

The information contained in this book has been compiled from sources deemed reliable, and it is accurate to the best of the Author's knowledge; however, the Author cannot guarantee its accuracy and validity and cannot be held liable for any errors or omissions. Changes are periodically made to this book. You must consult your doctor or get professional medical advice before using any of the suggested remedies, techniques, or information in this book.

Upon using the information contained in this book, you agree to hold harmless the Author from and against any damages, costs, and expenses, including any legal fees potentially resulting from the application of any of the information provided by this guide. This disclaimer applies to any damages or injury caused by the use and application, whether directly or indirectly, of any advice or information presented, whether for breach of contract, tort, negligence, personal injury, criminal intent, or under any other cause of action.

You agree to accept all risks of using the information presented inside this book. You need to consult a professional medical practitioner in order to ensure you are both able and healthy enough to participate in this program.

Table of contents

Introduction 1

Chapter 1: Protection Of Pilgrims 3

Chapter 2: Warriors Who Have Been Trained To Fight 10

Chapter 3: A Third Battle For Jerusalem. 23

Chapter 4: Threats And Changes 36

Chapter 5: Suspicions, Accusations And Suspicions 44

Chapter 6: When The Templars They Fall 54

Chapter 7: What Are The Templars And What Are They? 57

Chapter 8: Pilgrimages, And The First Crusade 66

Chapter 9: Campaigning In Outremer .. 105

Chapter 10: The Chinon Parchment 137

Chapter 11: The Interpretation Of The Evidence 164

Conclusion 181

Introduction

First Knights Templar appeared in 1129 and the establishment of their Order. They quickly spread across the Christian world, gaining influence and power. They played an important part in the Crusades and in protecting Christian pilgrims and warriors in their journey to Jerusalem and gaining substantial economic power throughout the time. A large part of their financial power was their ability to create early models of banking.

But their banking and financial successes eventually led to a significant degree of jealousy on that of time's leaders, who were envious of the Templars for their influence and power. Rumours of secret initiations sparked the atmosphere of fear and suspicion around the Templars and the king of France, Philip IV, was determined to get away from the massive obligations he owed the Order by having many of its members detained, tortured, and executed. The Order was closed, however, rumors persist to today about their fate and assets. They are also featured in popular literature like the 'DaVinci Code'.

Chapter 1: Protection Of Pilgrims

At the beginning of the 10th century AD, Jerusalem was in danger. Jerusalem was the center of intense fighting because of its significance to religion. It was believed that the Ark of the Covenant was delivered to the city under the reign of King David which made it an Holy City to Jews. Christians were of the belief the belief that Jerusalem would be Jerusalem as the Holy City upon Christ's return to Earth. Jerusalem was also the site of Mohammad's ascension into Heaven and was considered to be the second most important place in the Islamic religion.

Three major religions believed that the city belonged to them. They also believed that the Christians gained control over the city from Muslims in the summer of 1099. It was, naturally an element of the Crusades which was a long bloody, dramatic battle that fought between Christians as well as Muslims. In the crusade that was first, as in other crusades, knights, peasants and even serfs joined forces for the Christian cause in order to take on Muslim forces. The use of shields and swords was common in medieval battles fashion, along with catapults and battering-rams. Cities were under siege during months of stretch and conditions of surrendering to the city defeated was commonplace.

The Christian forces launched an awe-inspiring, brutal attack of innocent civilians all over the city, which made it splattered in blood. Then they had to take on the job of establishing the city as a Christian city, establishing the right leadership as well as getting Jerusalem back to its feet in the new age. It was a time of change for Jerusalem. Christian Crusaders were now a quite a distance away from the lands of their Western European homes, in possession of not only Jerusalem and its surrounding areas, but also territories they had conquered throughout their journey. They named the road which led to England through England to Jerusalem outremer, which was the Outremer, French for "across the ocean," and it was comprised of smaller fiefdoms like Edessa as well as Tripoli.

So, even though The First Crusade had been for the goal of securing the sought-after Holy Land, it also offered an association made up of European Christians (the Crusading forces comprised of Christians from a variety of Western European nations) a new set of territory to oversee.

A few villages were as strewn pebbles on the Outremer the Outremer was used predominantly as a route for Christian pilgrims who wanted to make it to Jerusalem and ask for to be forgiven for their wrongs. It was an intriguing and fascinating mix of wandering bands from all classes, nationalities and faiths, with different motives.

If there were people who were traveling There would be bandits. There were also marauders and slave traders. Pilgrims were given gifts to place on an altar in Jerusalem and residents of the Eastern regions (of what we now call Middle-Eastern heritage Some Muslim and others not) made the most of it.

Kidnappings, robberies, and attacks occurred frequently however in some instances they were not individual they were on a large scale. On the Easter of 1119, a crowd of seven hundred pilgrims were looking for the well-known baptismal place of Christ in the vicinity of Jericho leaving Jerusalem. They were abducted off the coast of Jaffa by Fatimid rebels who killed half the group and then sold the rest to slaves.

In this particular set of circumstances came the secular knights. Knights were adventurers as well as professional soldiers who signed contracts for specific periods that included military services. They were granted property and people to assist them and, most importantly, cash. They were, naturally large, strong and courageous, looking for the post because of their desire to explore. They typically lived lives of leisure with such indulgences as they were presented with.

Over the course of several years, Jerusalem was not just the most frequent pilgrimage destination but also was becoming more populated and transforming into a functioning metropolis, the question of how to safeguard the people who were visiting it was studied. It was in 1119 that it was that the Knights Templar were formally created.

Nine knights were provided with lodgings at the royal palaces of the King Baldwin II, located in the northern part of the Temple of the Lord. They were dressed in secular attire and were assigned a general list of duties to guard the highway between Jaffa towards Jerusalem and to ensure that pilgrims were in a safe environment.

The names of the initial nine included: Hugues De Payen the Godefroid of Saint-Omer Andre de Motbard, Godefroy, Roral, Gundomar, Geoffrey Bisol, Payen de Motdesir, and Archambaud de Saint Aignan.

The world of the time was controlled by a slew of titles, patronages, and positions in life that are difficult for us to understand through this volume. However groups such as those of the Templars had always needed funds and authority. Though they were originally housed in the castle of the King however, this didn't grant the order an obvious position as one would expect. Therefore, the first members had to work hard to establish their place on the list of rank.

The Knights needed at a minimum subventions to cover their operating costs. The historian John J. Robinson tells us that the subsidies included two horses, an person to assist them with their armor, their own armor as well as food, weapons, and various other costs.

Robinson further reveals we that Knights Templar along with other knights, were able to pocket the money they earned while battling bandits, but an important source of income was always a major issue. The Templars won an early victory in this regard after a request for help was received by the rich judge of Champagne. He gave the Order the land at Troyes and served as an example to follow for their operations over the years.

In time the estates would earn funds through the sales of farm products, as well as bakeries and mills. The Knights would have ample funds to pay for expenses and would transfer the excess to Jerusalem.

When they began to work under the aegis of Champagne the Knights were able to experience a major change. They had to transition from their current knighthood to an order of religious significance. This meant that they had to cut out some of the more intriguing elements of their stories and re-establishing their lives in a manner that could associate with monks regardless of whether it was a standard for knights of the religious order.

The fascinating combination of man and warrior of God discovered a middle place in the Knights concept of chivalry. It is essentially what is what the Western world sees it to be in the present. It meant being a helper to people who needed help and being kind in certain situations and, when they weren't fighting and being a gentleman. Also, wearing a stylish outfit.

Also, the order had a distinct order of things, where there was a grandmaster the top of the hierarchy. Every sovereign state with an order was governed by an "master," who would rule without a grandmaster. Like one would expect, the members of the order were subject to laws of the territory where they resided. Once they were established the time was right for Knights Templar to begin earning the fame they would eventually enjoy.

Chapter 2: Warriors Who Have Been Trained To Fight

The Templars were regarded by the past as great warriors and the main source of their fame lies in their education. They were a well-organized group of soldiers, trained in the art of fighting in unison. This was the most advanced method of the time. In the era of pell mell combat in the 18th century, the Templars were taught to obey orders.

They came together around a battle standard known as the Beauseant. It was not just the title of an item, it was rather a phrase that meant "be elegant!" or "be glorious!" When the troops were spread out during battle, they would look for this horizontal banner strewn between two rods vertically and gather around it.

The information on the Knights their early battles and activities isn't complete However, we do have an idea of of their early combative activities. One battle in the early days was part of a cause commanded by Raymond II, Count of Tripoli and Fulk V, who was reigning as Kings of Jerusalem at the time. They were enlisted in the fight to an antagonist known as Imad the Zengi. Zengi was a fierce atabeg (governor) of Mosul and, during the year 1137, Mosul sacked to the city of Homs that was later taken over by Damascus.

The Templars were summoned to join forces with Raymond and Raymond, who were to pursue Zengi towards Zengi's home, the Orontes valley, which was the site of an outpost from Tripoli. The newly formed order of Knights suffered one of its first sour losses when Zengi's soldiers attacked them by surprise, and took a number of Knights hostage. The remaining Knights tried a plan of hiding in the Frankish castle in Montferrand in the direction that Zengi was originally moving when he threw them a curveball. They were spotted by Zengi in a flash and quickly forced their castle under attack.

One of the most difficult issues the Franks confronted while they were huddled under the attack was that they'd sneaked into the fortress in such a hurry that they'd forgotten their provisions. They'd caused themselves near-starvation and were forced to eat their horses. In essence, the 18 captive Templars were part of the largest Frankish group who surrendered without being aware of the large number of law enforcement officers coming their way. They were allowed to go by releasing the city.

The Muslim world continued to batter the numerous settlements in the Outremer but some relief following Zengi's 1145 killing within his tent. However, Frankish leaders were worried at the loss of the garrisons of their troops and they re-energized their troops for what would be The Second Crusade.

They were enlisted into an army commanded under the reign of Louis VII, the King of France. Louis VII, who seemed to think of himself as the one who erected an army to protect against adversaries more than an element of the Christian Crusade. In any case the western contingent from the Templars (who are now scattered all over the Outremer) participated in a conference in the Paris Temple in April 1147 hosted by King Louis and the pope Eugenius III.

It was determined to decide that Knights Templar would be part of Louis the fighting force. It was also agreed to march into battle in a new uniform. This was among the most distinct of their designs in addition to being one of their most renowned aspects of their history. They were provided with white robes that featured the distinctive red cross at the center that would make them instantly famous.

The Knights Templar set out with the remainder of the Crusade with the help of their French Preceptor Everard de Barres. They rode alongside German soldiers, and eventually were recognized in their discipline and competence. In one incident, Germans were compelled to stop and wash their horses and themselves after seeing the Knights doing the same. The enemies Seljuk army was quick to attack, severely crippling the army. But, the majority or all of the Knights were able to escape.

They naturally gained their respect from the French command. Louis quickly appointed an Templar to lead his army, Everard des Barres, head of the French Temple. In the manner that Michael Haag outlines, des Barres believed that an organization was the primary step to success, and his troops were divided into groups of fifty with the Templar Knight taking on the huge task of commanding this group. In this context the Knights had advanced beyond being a police unit that stopped thieves in the road to Jerusalem.

Under the direction of des Barres as well as the fifty individuals who ruled The Knights brought back another element of Roman culture that was lost in the dark ages. They also created an effective army that was organized. Des Barres helped develop a uniformity of the archers' positions and other elements of the force which ensured consistency and efficient.

A Templar could not, as outlined by Edward Burman, quit the Templars without permission in the event of an emergency except for the rescue of the life of a Christian who was in danger from being shot by an "Moslem."

In the second crusade the Templars also served as fundraisers, farming and other business generating money that they put into their fellow French troops of which they formed a part. Haag informs us that this amount was more than 50% of France's annual tax revenues.

But, the outcome and victory in battle were out of their hands, as the second crusade sank quickly, followed by a decisive smack at Damascus. The humiliating defeat was trapped in dense orchards, and being sprayed with the arrows. Similar to what had occurred earlier there was a part of the troops, commanded by Baldwin himself Baldwin himself - was also tucked into a specific area in the town of Damascus separated from their resources and being pounded to submission.

The remainder of the crusade was comprised of minor, ineffectual battles that had no significant consequences, without any debits to the part of Frankish forces. The result was that they were less fortunate than they were the Outremer prior to this, and the bulk of the next few years were dominated by Muslim controlling the area. The situation grew more pronounced and ferocious under the guidance of the above-mentioned powerful warrior Saladin.

It was under Saladin's rule and the career of Saladin when the Templars were given opportunities and responsibility for protecting regions that were part of Outremer. They were Christians (Franks) were still in the supreme territory of Jerusalem and were pleased with their position, but they have to control the Muslims or gain some of the forces in the Outremer.

One of the factors was the building of a castle in Chastellet that would be popularly known as Jacob's Ford. Templars thought of this embattlement and identified its location. It was built in Muslim territory, and was the sole place that humans could traverse over the River Jordan in that general region.

It was a huge rectangular structure made of stone and in 1179, at mid-construction was headed to becoming the largest fortress known world. Saladin made the enthralling decision of providing Baldwin the sum of 100,000 in exchange for the right to stop construction and to demolish the structure. If Baldwin refused to accept the offer in a negative response, Saladin accepted the opportunity to test the demolition himself.

After a brief attack on The city's walls, Saladin's army started tearing it down in the course of destroying the walls of one of the walls over just a few days. They gained entry and they took prisoners and killed hundreds of them. Saladin himself, following his usual practice, was able to witness the killing personally. Many of the dead were Templars and Saladin's commander gave his life to the cause by fleeing in the flames that erupted from the smoldering city.

The Muslims made use of the wealth in the city and then toppling it was an amazing declaration. It changed the course of events to the benefit of Saladin's Muslim forces. It was only the haphazard occurrence of a drought assisted the Franks. The natural disaster caused Saladin to be able to accept slowing down his attack after Baldwin came to a peace agreement. The truce allowed both sides to pursue their own goals and allowed traders to move through areas that had previously were too war-ravaged to be secure. The truce was shattered through Raynald from Chatillon, the lord of Oultrejourdain who was the commander of an army that pillaged goods from the Muslim caravan that was heading towards Damascus.

In addition, Raynald sacked Arabian in addition to Egyptian ports and suffered the price when his navy forces were defeated by forces of al-Adil Saladin's brother. Al-Adil killed all prisoners he held that the west saw as an indication that Saladin wished to spread the jihad of Saladin across Frankish nations.

After this an additional event occurred which pushed the animosity between the two parties to the edge. Baldwin IV died, leaving Baldwin V as boy king and Raymond from Tripoli as the Regent. A complicated and contentious procedure was followed after Baldwin V died in August of 1186. Eventually the Princess Sibylla was made Queen. She later married Guy of Lusignan who was the stepfather of Baldwin V, who then was crowned King.

Reynald, who's previous raids of merchant caravans didn't go over well, thought it was about time to do another. He jumped off a massive caravan headed to Damascus and killed the majority of the Egyptian soldiers acting as guards as well as killing a handful of merchants and civilians as well as selling the rest as slaves. Reynald brought his enormous wealth back to Kerak and waited for the fury of his arch-nemesis Saladin.

Saladin could have been expected to unleash his anger in the form of hundreds of soldiers with swords However, he appointed an envoy to Reynald to discuss the release of the prisoners. Reynald did not want to honor the request by denying it which is why he sent diplomatic envoys directly to King Guy.

King Guy struck an agreement, but it was contingent on Reynald to sign the truce, and when Reynald didn't, he created an unavoidable division throughout the realm. Meanwhile, Raymond of Tripoli came up with an alliance which would include Saladin in helping Raymond establish himself as the King of Jerusalem following Saladin's likely victory in the battle.

Then, the Saladin pleaded with to persuade the traitor Raymond to let him send a scouting group through Galilee. Raymond warned that the group, who were slaves, would be passing through and the inhabitants should remain inside. The moment Grandmaster Gerard de Ridefort learned of this, he was adamant that the best way to take on the Muslims without their protection.

He did it in a small group of around a hundred and at the summit of the ridge saw him staring into the barrel of thousands of Muslim troops. Templar James de Mailly was the commander of the troops and he was determined to quit. This was not accepted by de Ridefort, who urged troops to join the battle.

In the end, bloodshed ensued which was followed by a bloodbath, and Mailly was swiftly killed. The remaining Templars in the fight, except for three, which included de Ridefort, perished as well. The citizens of Nazareth were enslaved.

Saladin was believed to be marching yet again. After their terrible journey at Nazareth the Frankish forces needed to regroup to defend. They set up a Camp at Sephoria. From there, they had to trek to Tiberieas where the there was a Countess Eschiba was under attack by inadequate troops. De Ridefort prevailed upon King Guy to send troops there to assist.

Along the way, they came to the twin peaks of rock that are known as The Horns of Hattin. After settling in, some of the men, thirsty from their long journey in the heat, rushed to fetch water from the lake, which was swiftly destroyed by Muslims. Saladin ignited nearby brushes which emitted a thick smoke into the camp, making it difficult for soldiers to breathe.

In the early morning, Frankish soldiers set off against Saladin's troops, putting in an effort to fight an intense battle, yet they were defeated. John J. Robinson tells us that, at the close to the war, Saladin informed his troops eager to rejoice, "we have not beaten them until the tent (of King Guy) is destroyed." After the words came from his mouth were heard by the tent that was blown away.

The top leaders of the Frankish forces were taken into custody and taken to Saladin's tent to discuss negotiations. Saladin was quick to light on his arch-enemy, Reynald of Chatillon, the caravan raider who broke the truce. In the course of the argument Saladin cut into Reynald using his sword, and killed the slain man. Other leaders were rounded up and ransomed.

But it was the Knights Templar were to suffer one of their most horrific fates and most humiliating of all, the humiliation. There were hundreds in captivity and Saladin was particularly cruel. He was fighting or not Saladin was being accompanied by Egyptian Sufis and believed he should let them witness the act of beheading the captives. The ceremony went horribly by the Sufis trying their best to be pleasing their hosts, only to be mocked when they took several awkward steps to perform their terrible act. Imagine hundreds of beheadings in the presence of De Ridfort.

Chapter 3: A Third Battle For Jerusalem

De Ridfort was spared beheading at the conclusion of Battle of Hattin, instead being taken as a prisoner. Grand preceptor Terricus fled on his own and was able to write his knights in the company to explain the devastation. However, he also wrote about something else which was more significant to the Franks in the larger picture and that was the manner in which the Muslims were cutting across the Outremer by tearing down garrisons like Acre, Sidon, and Jaffa. There was only Beirut, Tyre, Ascalon as well as Jerusalem had remained.

De Ridfort was offered freedom in exchange for peacefully surrendering the Templar garrison in Gaza. Although Templar rules prohibited ransoms in exchange in exchange for money, they didn't prohibit this kind of deal however, which was far more serious and unsettling. Because of the rules of obedience of a governing authority The remaining Knights in Gaza were required to surrender when requested from De Ridfort.

The Templars had seen a decline of half their population in the region and they had no garrisons that were fully operational. For the Holy City itself, it was absorbing huge numbers of refugees however, it was in dire the need of Knights to defend it. Bailan of Ibelin Archbishop of Tyre came to Tyre and started knighting teenagers who had no knowledge or training in the military.

The Muslims came in swiftly and immediately began digging tunnels into the city of gold. Their guards rushed into the city and began to assault the wall that the Christians were able to defend with great force. The attack was simple and simple, but also effective. an intentional tearing down which quickly convinced the residents of the city that they were in danger. The only thingthat, from a strategic perspective to consider, that the Christians could boast of was the fact that they held, within the town they controlled Muslim prisoners.

This was helpful in talks to end the siege that Balian began shortly after it was broken. Instead of letting the Muslims continue to batter and violent battles the leader offered to surrender the city, using the spooky bargaining chip of the lives of Muslims living in the city. It wasn't enough, so Saladin and he came up with to come up with the ransom of Muslims within Jerusalem.

Saladin waited for two days to actually get into the city, so that the grand victory could be celebrated on the 2nd of October which was the day to remember the Prophet Muhammad who was taken to his burial place on the Temple Mount, which is what was designated Jerusalem as the 3rd holy city within Islam. Secretary of Saladin Imad al-Din wrote that the Sultan's face "shone with happiness" when he entered the city. The process of when the city is changed hands because of conquering isn't without ceremony. Saladin's troops made a mad dash to at the Temple Mount, removing the Christian artifacts and demolishing structures, like as the church of Augustinian canons. In the end, the Dome of the Rock was crushed in front of remaining Franks and a shout in the form of "Allah is Great!" ran through the city that was conquered.

Queen Sibylla was permitted to go out of the city without having to pay ransom, however all other residents needed an invoice for payment, and the evacuation was complete in November. 10 , 1187.

It was clear that the loss of Jerusalem was a massive hit to the Franks. However, life was not over, and that meant facing the tough realities of dealing with Muslim advancement and protecting their only remaining land, Tyre. Conrad, the Lord of Tyre was proactive in his approach and enlisted Tyre's Knights Templar to attack Saladin's naval forces. The Templar-led Frankish forces took over several ships as well as the admiral-in-chief of Alexandria.

Feeling irritable, and noticing his resources were stretched, Saladin slowed down his activities a bit. Although he destroyed the church in Tortosa but he was not keen on taking on the city itself, a Templar stronghold as in that of the Templar castle located in Safita. In exchange for this reprieve, Franks actually took on the task of recapturing of the town of Acre.

In this pivotal battle that was fought, the Templars took on Kurdish forces from Diyarbakir and were able to reduce their number in order to launch an obscene assault on Acre. The Muslim forces in the city were more than double the strength of the attackers. King Guy was excited about the possibilities and was able to get de Ridfort in charge as the leader.

Incredibly, this surge occurred simultaneously with the fervor was growing for the crusades in general and the small group of Templar-led Franks were with forces from a variety of countries of the West-Central Europe. The largest of these fleets to join the crusades was one of a German group with the ferocious fighter Frederick Barbarossa. This bearded crusader was a descendant from the Hohenstausen dynasty. In the past, he enjoyed earned a reputation for being a world-class conqueror, and was designated Holy Roman Emperor in exchange for fighting enemies in the name of Pope Adrian IV.

Barbarossa led his forces to Acre together with other troops they were preparing for battle. Conrad of Monferrat who was the commander of the overall forces and noticed the fact that his troops were losing the control. This, along with the unstable mental state of his troops in Rid fort, posed an obvious risk to the Franks.

With the various groups of crusaders they were able to gather numbers. After repelling an initial attack from Saladin--no easy feat, they rallied themselves and were ready to take on Saladin. Both sides fought swords, resulting in men being slain and the terrible cry of combat. No matter how much passion or fury one of the soldiers generated, their efforts as well as their blood accumulated to a deadlock and the Christian forces being the first to take refuge within their garrisons.

If they had done this,, Gerard de Rid fort at war, battle-tested, and awed and descending into madness did not change. He remained on the field and the others around him were withdrawn, refusing to go away unless it was an unbeatable victory.

The exhausted Muslim forces looked at each other, asked one another what the man was doing, the man was taken prisoner. From the many choices available to Saladin to receive the treatment of the Grand Master, the sultan opted for execution. They were the Knights Templar were without head, as he had basically executed himself. While historians and commentators as well as other groups discussed the Templars through the centuries, this odd action would prompt critiques and negative depictions.

For the battle on Acre It continued. And on. The particular battle caused a number of casualties, but little result. However, the Christians took the fight to pieces in the midst of the intriguing ways of the past the battle of Acre was incorporated into the Third Crusade. The precepts of Europe served as a place of training for Knights to take to Acre as well as for other areas that were part of the Crusade. Richard Lionheart also arrived with troops as did the former friend Robert from Sable was made to be the grand master of the Templars. This dynamic duo along with the other troops led to the acceptance of Acre against Saladin. After some confusion as to how the men reached an agreement on and after the Frankish troops arrived in Acre, Richard took 2,700 Muslims out of the city and executed the Muslims. This was revenge for Saladin's brutality against Franks who he defeated in Hattin and other nations.

The Franks then embarked to the extreme of taking back some of the cities and areas Saladin had conquered during The second Crusade. The process of gaining against such an elite fighting force was no simple accomplishment, and it didn't take long before Saladin had rallied and was ready for an enormous fight. It took place in Arsuf, a town in the region of Arsuf on September. 7 1191.

The Christian Army, part of the forces of Richard Lionheart, and Saladin's army, came together on a vast plain just outside the city. They were Christians together with the Sea in their backs. The Templars formed the right-hand side of the group. In front of them were a group of bowmen as well as spearmen who helped to keep Muslim bowmen from their range. The Christians took on a defensive role trying to bend, but not break, after Bedouin soldiers rushed at them. Turkish horses swarmed with scimitars.

For knights as well as soldiers of all kinds standing steady as you wait for your opponent to tire itself out is an method which requires an extraordinary amount of patience. The Hospitallers were a unit that was that had a similar mission and origins to the Templars were defending in the back when one of their troops even though they were under similar to the Templars the obligation not to move without a directive they did exactly that, speeding forward, and bringing Flemish forces along with the group. The result was a ripple effect in which a whole column swarmed into the gap, including all the assembled Templars.

Although this action was not ordered however, it proved effective in dispersing Muslim riders, the overwhelming majority of them fought an accelerated retreat. This one, impromptu attack was a win for the Christians. The Muslims were spared, as Richard was warned not to pursue an advancing Muslim army because one of their strategies was to make it appear that they were retreating to create an opening for the forces that were pursuing them.

The capture of Acre was a huge victory for Christians as was they were hoping that the Third Crusade, nearing its conclusion, was poised to be a huge success. While they had not yet reclaimed Jerusalem but the Franks had transformed out the Outremer into a predominantly Christian collection of strongholds on the coast. They also enjoyed a time of peace with Muslims.

The year 1193 was the time that Saladin was killed and greatly strengthened Saladin's Christian position. The empire was thrown into chaos, and the Christians enjoyed prioritization in the Outremer in either preparing to take back Jerusalem or having peace.

In this context, Acre became the city where emigrants from Jerusalem were able to go to, which was a kind of Capital of that Christian world. Acre also became the capital city of the Templars. They constructed a massive fortification along the coast to the southwest part of the city.

The Knights were now an integral part of protecting Christians in their land as before. One of the main reasons for this was the appointment Innocent III to the positon of Pope. Edward Burman writes that Innocent was thought to be the possessor with "iron spirit and extreme religious conviction" in addition to the fact that Innocent wished to use these qualities to "the establishment of a feudal government founded on an absolute authority in the Church." Burman further ventures that this ambition was "the the highest level of the authority in the early medieval Roman Church."

Enter the Templars who, on behalf of Innocent would issue not less as fifty papal bulls throughout his time. The pope regarded the Knights as a militia, but they also relied on their fundraising abilities. It was a period of diplomatic and political power for the Templars as well as a period that saw the construction of huge new castles, like Baghras that had bigger and stronger walls towers, moats and moats and ramparts.

In 1210 in 1210, the Templars chose William d Chartres as their Grand Master, which was the 14th to be elected in the history. John of Brienne was the new King of Jerusalem and enjoyed a close relationship with the Templars. The Templars put their fundraising machines to begin a new campaign to start in 1217. The plan included a tax that was to be paid by the Templars and supervised by the pope of the moment, Honorius III, who succeeded Innocent after his death in July of 2016.

In the new war the Templars were involved in a way other than fighting. One of their duties was to assist in the development of a new defensive model for Christians and Muslims, which the Muslims will have to adapt to. They selected as their place of residence for this mission a point known as Athlit, a sliver of land that stretches three-quarters of a mile deep into the sea and is surrounded by rocks. For many years it was believed that the Templars had the watchtower at Destroit, but decided to enhance it with a wall that was built on the natural defense of the sea and rocks.

They built an improvement on Baghras the fortress of a great size known as Chastel Pelerin, Castle Pilgrim. The wall that surrounded the stronghold was 16 feet thick and 90 feet high. The walls were awash with hundreds of people. it's important to mention that this fortress city also provided livestock, orchards and the fish pond.

The stronghold will be due to its location equipped with support forces and supplies by maritime rather than on land, which makes it more difficult for Muslims to stop these essential aids. This significant change in defense was an immediate reaction to the roads at Acre as well as Tyre. There was also speculation that the fortress was a means to allow the Templars to escape the sins committed by Acre. Acre.

Without Saladin on the scene the castle was given to an Al-Mu'azzam, a new Sultan the ruler of Damascus and Damascus, who put the castle through the first chance to test. In the course of Al-Mu'azzam's attack grand master Pedro de Montaigu and his 300 soldiers were safe within the fortress they had constructed. It was battered and thrown rocks by the Muslims and stood solid for a month until the enemies made a decision to abandon.

The Templars have proven their strength as builders, warriors and military strategists. But their power was, as usual, uncertain.

Chapter 4: Threats And Changes

The Knights Templar were established for a particular goal and have prospered over two centuries with an increased and expanding function. Due to various reasons, such as King of Jerusalem following King of Jerusalem after King of Jerusalem as well as Pope and Pope continued going on and that made it necessary to the Templars.

However, in the month of March of 1229 Frederick II became King of Jerusalem and, while he was a crusader he was not convinced of importance in the Templars. This was because of an argument among pope Gregory and Frederick which put the Templars in an uneasy political environment. The Pope had crusades in his mind for Frederick but not ones that matched with the Emperor's (he was also called"the Holy Roman Emperor" Holy Roman Emperor) master plans, which were developed partly by different treaties with Sultans. Frederick did not hesitate to defy the pope, resulting in not just one, but two excommunications.

Remember, the Knights of Columbus were an order of religious faith and adhered to their rules of conduct. Therefore when Frederick was invited to Acre to meet they had no other choice other than to refuse him entry to the city according to the instructions of Gregory.

When Frederick embarked on his crucial march, whether to attempt to conquer Jerusalem or try a kind of diplomacy, he enlisted the Templars to accompany with him. This would, obviously represent a defiance of Gregory and The Grand Master de Montaigu was unable to do. However, he did not wish to sit and watch Christian brothers put their lives at risk in battle. He did not want to be ignored or penalized by Frederick.

The Templars have come up with an odd compromise in which they actually participated in the Frederick campaign but attempted to justify themselves by using an exemption by remaining a day behind during the march, which meant they didn't march alongside Frederick technically.

When the stragglers got gained ground to the others, they weren't happy with the information they received. Frederick was in talks with Sultan Al-Kamil and incredible success in negotiating the acquisition of Jerusalem to the Christians. The city was now functioning as a pilgrimage destination but was not a major concern to Al-Kamil with the exception of some isolated Muslim holy sites. In accordance with the agreement theseplaces, including those of the Temple Mount, the Dome of the Rock and several other places were, in some way, to remain controlled by Muslims, while the remainder could be handed over to Christians with the condition that it was not protected.

The result was not a pleasant one for the Templars who naturally, did not have a say on the issue. De Montaigu was outraged about the one area of Jerusalem that was going to remain in Muslim control that was the al-Aqsa Mosque. Although this structure had undisputed significance to the Muslim faith, for Montaigu it was of great value in the sense that it was the structure it was Baldwin II had given to the Templars at the time of their founding. the patriarch from Jerusalem had a similar opinion and put Jerusalem under interdict. Jerusalem under the interdict.

This sequence of events led to the Templars an accusation of treason against Frederick who, at the time, favored the countrymen's order known as "the Teutonic Knights. In addition, with a vindictiveness that is sometimes attributed to an emperor Frederick was able to steal the Chastel Pelerin away from the Knights Templar and give this valuable item to the Teutonic Knights. But it was those knights, who had actually visited the castle, who swayed into letting their boss off of this sham. Based on Robinson, Frederick next entertained the idea of kidnapping de Montaigu as a means of destroying the structure, however neither plan did anything. But, it definitely seems like a threatening prelude to the tendency of certain groups to conspire to take on the Knights.

The next decade was filled with losses and gains for the Templars in addition to changes in power. The Templars lost Grand Masters and gained new ones. The Pope and the other leaders were elected and gone but one thing that was constant was that the enthusiasm for crusading had cooled off for years on end.

In 1248 In 1248, the Templars under the direction from St. Louis of France was merged with the Hospitallers. The reason behind this was the increased enthusiasm for the crusade in the wake of its demise. The forces that were gathered were believed to be necessary in order to recapture Jerusalem. But, the position of pope was changed hands for more than a century following this union. The philosophical enthusiasm for the reconquest of Jerusalem might have existed however, it was not the leadership.

The crusades always had the apparent purpose of capturing and holding Jerusalem even though different campaigns were characterized by diversions. Naturally, Muslim sieges of various Christian strongholds weakened forces in general and delayed any attack on Jerusalem. This was the case for the Muslims who attacked Acre at the time of 1289.

One of the incidents that led to this loss was an incredibly violent act by an unnamed band of Venetian soldiers acting as part of Christian forces. The band, which was unpaid and loosely grouped, engaged in an argument with Muslim civilians that turned into a massive, bloody protest. Families of the murdered Muslims carried their loved ones' blood-stained clothes to Sultan Kala'un who promised to take revenge on them.

The Templars Chief Master, William de Beaujeu, demanded that the soldiers who had committed the offense be turned over to Muslims to ensure that the repercussions of their outrage should be Acre. Acre. Some skeptics put this down as a concern about certain aspects of the Templars business relations with Muslims. It was always the norm that, regardless of religious affiliation or not in it was the case that Mediterranean was the center of trade that was rich and flowing both ways, with strong financial connections between Christian or Muslim groups, as well as between those living in countries that adhered to these religions.

In other words it was not a good idea in surrendering to Muslims and certainly not in preparing for a siege on Acre in the time de Beaujeu had warned of one being imminent. When the siege actually did occur and was awe-inspiring and claimed more than 1000 lives. If men of the adult age were not killed the siege, it was due to an oversight. As the siege was nearing its dreadful finality, the commander of the Muslim forces, al-Ashraf

Khan approached the Templar responsible for Acre, Peter de Severy with terms to facilitate the Christians to surrender. In exchange for this surrender the lives of all in Acre would be spared. the Templars were able to keep their weapons and bring along with them anything they could carry.

However, once the gates opened, Mamelukes came in as Christians began to walk out, Mameluke army began rape girls and women. Knights Templar did not allow the rapes, and came back with a counter-attack that took down every Mameluke present. The knights then blocked the gate , and the flag of the Sultan was lowered. The fighting was not over.

In the morning, the sultan arranged for an embassy in the morning to apologize for the crimes committed by Mamelukes. He requested a diplomatic group of Christians to come to his meeting. This group was comprised from de Severy and the various Knights who he chose to accompany his. In case the tone apology offered by Khalil seemed too appealing to be authentic It was.

The sultan and his comrades weren't there to offer apologies but as soon as the Knights arrived they were attacked and killed. In the midst of this in the background, the Muslims were constructing tunnels underneath Acre's city. Acre. They burned the foundations beneath and then set fire to Acre's city. They quickly took over the city, then moved further to Tyre. The Christians were devastated by their loss.

Chapter 5: Suspicions, Accusations And Suspicions

Like the entire culture The Templars' religion incorporated some quantity of ritual. The privilege to perform certain rituals may be seen as favoritism, and create some resentment. For instance the Templars did not adhere to the standard Catholic custom by burying the bodies of those who were excommunicated as well as by burying a portion of their deceased in their personal cemeteries.

Innocent III, whose time as Pope was marked by an increase in the responsibilities of the Templars, issued an uncompromising rebuke of them in 1207 for their burial rituals. The alleged violations of privilege or power were blamed on an inability to be humble, an attribute that Pope Clement also scolded the Templars in the 13th century. He also believed that the Order was too focused on earning funds and was able to recruit its members (who pay dues) in a manner that was not respectful of their fellow members.

The most successful groups will withstand the toughest critiques and suspicions. this turned out to be a dire warning for the Templars as they became less significant after the fall Acre. The crusades, despite generating some fanfare in certain quarters but were generally in disrepute in the period of time as the defeats they suffered recently not being enough to inspire.

One could claim that, in the face of some of the troubles that plagued the Christian world The Templars could be a target of blame. Things started to go against the Templars as they discovered that the French Monarch of the time (the beginning of the 14th century), Philip IV, was in financial trouble. Clement V, the Pope at the time, wasn't an effective or strong supporter of the Templars. Their situation was unstable.

Philip confessed to Pope Clement during the latter's pope's coronation ceremony at the coronation of Pope Clement, that he had heard strange reports of the Templars performing initiation ceremonies which required young Knights to kiss buttocks and thighs of already established members. Then, he began putting the spies inside temples, and was soon able to file charges.

The Inquisition was in place by the time of this and had essentially an official list of witch hunt tactics through which people accused of heresy could not have any recourse to defend themselves. The Inquisition, invoking this strategy, Philip had many Templars taken into custody on October. 13th and 1307.

The accusations against them were all of heresy. Some of them were the worst. serious was the claim that certain Templars after joining to the Order, spat at the Christ image. Christ that Philip believed was as a second crucifixion. Another charge stemmed from the initiation-rites accusations and claimed that members were naked , and kissed the senior officers of the Order. Also, it was claimed that throughout their time in the order Knights had to be in "carnal relationships" with one another.

The king ordered that every member of the order in every temple be detained and subjected to an inquiry. When the arrests were conducted on the 13th day of the week thirteen Knights were able to escape this means that the search of the men was successful in an extremely high rate.

The king claimed to have conferred with Pope Clement prior to making the arrests, but Pope Clement stated that he had not authorized any arrests. This may be a sign that he had acknowledged an event of some sort however he was not being accountable for the arrests.

However, as you can imagine it is likely that the Templars are shocked, and shocked by this abrupt, shocking attack on the Order. While the Knights were most well-known for their role in the field of combat, they did (as mentioned earlier) need to take care of the farming industry and other activities that were intended to construct the Templars important infrastructure.

The serene nature of the manor does not necessarily mean that the people who lived there could not have been guilty of a few crimes, just as or less than others. But, it is possible to see that the manor didn't appear to be the place for bizarre rituals or the intimidation of newcomers. In addition, the residents were not likely to believe that they would be trapped in a web of political intrigue and were not able to erect a violent stand should they choose to. They also were not the best candidates to be able to get out.

Along with arresting the Templars Philip's troops also seized not just weapons, money and money-making apparatus as well as the few items they could come up with that they believed could be used as evidence for heresy. John J. Robinson writes that, in the depressing collection, "A silver head was discovered with tiny bones it, which could be a relic of the Holy Trinity."

If Templars were actually prisoners or simply hunkered down at their homes and then became torture victims. According to Barber it was because of suffering from the strappado method of connecting the wrists of the victim and then attaching the wrists to a beam high and letting him hang in the air with arms displaced and put on a rack that has a windlass , which rotates the wrists and ankles to dislocate them, and holding flames close to their feet.

One Templar told me that looking at some of these tools led him to confess immediately. The confessions were all over the place.

When the interrogations and torture continued, a number of Templars were thrown into the air like dominoes. From the time of Oct. 21st, just one day after being arrested, a farm Templar known as Pierre Brocart confessed to spitting on the cross and sexual activity. Others who admitted to all of the above were later interrogated over idol worship.

When the trial began in Paris during September the initial set of interrogations focused on the one hundred and thirty-eight Templars who, out of them, 1003 confessed certain alleged crimes. Barber writes "Most Templars were concerned to be seen as innocent victimized by a system over that they had no say as they hoped to please their interrogators with an adequate confession." This led to their confessions to consist of illicit actions committed on them, often with the caveat that they were ineffective.

On the 24th of October. 24 On Oct. 24, the Grand master Jacque de Molay was subjected to an interrogation. Barber says that he behaved himself as "a terrified and confused man" and then told French officials precisely what they required. The story he told was that he'd received as a member of the Templars in the diocese of Autun in the year 1940. He was instructed to spit on the cross and did it. He claimed that when it was time to welcome his new colleagues, he carried the tradition in a manner that was indirect by not doing the act himself but stating that other members were expected to.

After the confession was made After that, authorities placed de Molay and other Templar leaders before an assembly of members in Paris. The date was October. 25. In the next meeting, de Molay repeated his confession, claiming that it was in the name of the other Templar leaders. He claimed he was misled by Satan and was reluctant to confess because of the consequences on Earth.

It's hard to tell the specifics of what aspects of de Molay's evidence were forced or orchestrated in what manner, and at what conditions however we know that he concluded his shocking Paris performance by writing an open letter to Templars in which he urged them to make the same confessions.

One who heeded this--or other--solicitations, was Humbert de Pairaud, whose title was Visitor of France, overseer of Templars throughout the country. His duties required him to go to chapters and houses that means he'd be believed to be aware of the happenings across France. He also presided over numerous "receptions," the rituals where these spittings as well as sexual assaults were believed to occur. A lot of Templars who admitted to such actions at the receptions cited Pairaud as the person personally responsible.

On the 9th of November, Pairaud admitted to the crimes of which were he accused. The Inquisitor attempted to pressure the pairaud to make as many confessions in the order as was possible. He convinced Pairaud to confess to having stroking an idol. Because he was second in command of the entire Order This was a slap for the Templars.

As the French crown had now the things it desired, the Templars properties and estates, and its financial troubles were generally cured. It was in need of the support of Pope Clement and received it in the shortest time. The pope established the mechanism to conduct further inquiries into the matter, including a pope's commission and provincial councils.

The Pope himself attending a gathering of around seventy Templars whom he believed to be guilty of disbelieving Christ However, he was not enraged by the kissing or other actions that were employed as initiation ceremonies are intended to scare new members and test their determination to stand up for the cause.

The year was 1308, and he subsequently was absolved in 1308, and he also absolved Jacque de Molay as well as other leaders. A significant part of the Templars tale was that the spitting of Christ wasn't intended in the way it seemed as a way to show the type of humiliation that one Knight would face if they were to be taken prisoner. However, the absolution this was granted wasn't publicized. As always in the past, the Templars were in a bind between religious and government authorities, since the Pope tried to stay clear of an open conflict with Philip.

Chapter 6: When The Templars They Fall

The absolution granted to a few Templars from Pope Clement was just the beginning. The focus was on investigating the individual Knights or the entire order. In 1310, frustrated by the lengthy process, Philip stepped things up by selecting Phillipe de Marigny, Archbishop of Sens as his council.

The Archbishop, as the as the head of the court proceedings against the Templars was in charge of several legal challenges, appeals and legal challenges. and caused the process to drag on. But, Philip now introduced a new kind of heresy charge which was directed at Templars who had changed their previous confessions. One group of fifty-four, for instance, were blasted until death on May, despite their innocence throughout.

The those in the Order to speak out for its cause, so the Templars gradually began to fall apart. They appeared to be feeling overwhelmed and helpless. Whatever code of conduct they might have adopted in general tems each man was his own in this case, and trying to avoid blame being the primary concern. Certain witnesses at the later trials began criticize everything they disliked about the Templars as well as the excessive ambition and pride.

The king took advantage of the chance to transform an advantage into an overwhelming victory. He sent his army to meet Pope Clement by threatening to leave the Templars. The pope later issued an official statement on Mar. 12, 1312 that stated it was abolishing the Temple and permanently halting the Templars the ability to become members or to carry out any of their duties. He declared that he would not permit anyone "to consider joining the order in the future or to wear or receive its uniform, or perform the role of an Templar."

If it was decided that the Knights Templar could remain in existence but they were forbidden from having a presence by the Pope and they there was no constitution or a structure that was backed by the church. They didn't have church protection as well, and had to take on their own when it came to government-sponsored harassment.

After their Order collapsed all around them Jacque De Molay as well as Geoffrey of Charney had grown tired of languishing in prisons since seven years. They decided to bring the issue to the forefront, insisting on their innocence and perhaps anticipating that this would result in them to be martyred. They were right. Two of them were taken to a tiny island and was burned to death to death at the stake. They could have believed that they were the final members of the Templars.

Chapter 7: What Are The Templars And What Are They?

Despite the suspicions King Philip claimed to have regarding the Templars however, they were never an underground society. Whatever they might or may not have accomplished by way of initiation rituals and rituals, everyone around them believed that they knew exactly what Templars were all about: cross-dressed Knights who were famous for their loyalty to their orders and leadership.

Through the years over the years, the Order would develop a semblance of secrecy or a sense of snobbery. People would ask what they were doing or what they were concealing, etc. They might be misled by Masons or other orders.

Certain histories of the Templars finish with their formal dissolution. There is no doubt that the Order maintained its existence in some way through the morphing of various orders that had different names and various mission.

One of them included that of the Order of Montesa. It was founded in 1317. Jaime II, King of Aragon established the order with the remaining lands of his country's Templars. The order did not only grant only properties that were ex-Templar as well as ex-Hospitaller territory. Similar to what was the case in the case of the original Knights Templar the disguise that the Order was to combat Muslims and Muslims, however this was in Valencia. The Order was absorbed by another that was a victim of tough times and was the Order of San Jorge de Alfansa. The name changed later to it's current name, the Order of Montesa and San Jorge de Alfansa.

In the 1350's, there was also a plan to merge the Order and the Hospitallers in the event that Peter IV was not impressed by the effectiveness of the Order's ability to combat Muslim forces. Then, Peter mounted an attack against Montesa like the one fought during the time of Philip to the Templars however it was less violent. Instead of formal charges of heresy or the brutal treatment that went along with these, Peter went the route of laying out charges, such as misusing the assets of the Order and non-compliance with rules of behavior and dress, as well as general inability to defend the frontier.

These charges led to the interrogation with individuals belonging to the Order. The report of the inquisitor, which was addressed to the King identified the misuse of funds by the nephews of the Master. Regarding the entire Order it was discovered that they were the use of money for "concubines," "bastards," and "whores." There was also price-gouging by masters who owned tenants.

One notary claimed to have heard an Order of the Knights Knight who was sarcastically declaring "look at how well-equipped to defend the frontier" that gave Peter just a little bit of what he had been searching for. One could also ask what the "frontier" required police protection in the first place, because it was noted that, as Larry J. Simon et the others note it was just one significant Muslim invasion from Morocco during the time of the order.

In the end, King Peter's scheme did not work The Order was not incorporated into the crown, and continued through its normal business. It was one of the tiniest details within the story of the Order. The Order would later aid in the fight against rebellious situation within Sardinia under the reign by King John I. It also assisted the King Alfonso V in his Neapolitan Campaigns. After a long time, and despite numerous instructions, Montesa was absorbed into the Crown by King Philip II, in 1587.

The other Order which grew direct from Templars is The Order of Christ, otherwise called The Order of Our Lord Jesus Christ. The Order of Christ was established not too long following the Order of Montesa, and its origins were in 1319. It was created in Portugal by King Dinis I. It took the Templars to Portugal and they lived there as refugees , however, they had an impressive reputation, wealth and responsibility. Since Portugal began it's Age of Discoveries, a period of immense exploration and expansion that it was during this time that the Templars prospered. This period saw Portugal becoming a major player in Africa as well as expanding trade in that manner. This was also the time of amazing sailors and sailing expeditions. the Templars were, in their turn wanted to discover an iconic city with glitter known as Prester John, the Christian kingdom in Prester John.

In the midst of the Crusades during the time that the Muslims were wreaking havoc throughout Frankish countries, many European officials were forced to seek the assistance of kingdoms located in Western Europe. One of them was Hugh Bishop of Jabala who pleaded with Pope Eugenius. He believed that the best way to secure assistance was to create an imaginary Prester John from his own side of the Tigris and then ask the Pope. The Prester John wrote an e-mail, in accordance with the legend created by Hugh who described the incredible gold and other treasures in his kingdom. It was enough to entice Eugenius and provide the assistance Hugh was seeking.

In the simplest terms, members belonging to members of the Order of Christ, well more than a century later embarked on sailing expeditions to search for this legendary kingdom. It's a romantic tale and a tale that is passed on. However, the stakes are raised when you consider that the famous explorationist Vasco da Gama part of the Order and an explorer of Prester John's realm.

His quest took him to Mozambique and he was unsuccessful.

But what is the story of Christopher Columbus? Was this controversial historical figure a part of this mysterious order? The history of the time tells us this answer to be "no." However the famous ships of his were sailing across the Americas with the famous distinctive red cross that is the symbol of Knights of Christ. Why? His father-in-law was an Knight and it's quite possible that Christopher acquired some information about navigation from him.

In the end, Henry the Navigator was Knight and the Knights were the ones responsible for Christianity spreading across Africa. Henry's men also occupied both the Canary as well as the Azores islands. There is a possibility that we'd have more information about their expeditions and also about the geography and the people that lived in those days if it wasn't for the confidentiality of the orders.

The Order lived many years of existence, extending until 1789 when the Queen Maria I of Portugal secularized the Order. There was no longer any Orders which were direct descendants of the Templars still in existence. But, this brought an exciting new era for the Templars that was one in which they were the subject of fantasy stories as well as a baffling and complicated collection of theories.

In the case of whether the Templars are similar to those of the Freemasons (Masonic Order Shriners,, etc.) The answer is a pretty clear "no." Evidence doesn't back up this assertion. It is mostly based on speculation regarding Members of the Order who moved to Scotland and establishing the Freemasons in Scotland.

Maybe through the accident of history and the passage of time, some novelists from the past were compelled to write novels featuring the Templars. Walter Scott placed a prominent victim in his novel Ivanhoe and Maurice Druon wrote a series which emphasized the mysterious nature of Templars. It is possible that the past could have treated them like monks, loyal servants to popes and monarchs as well. Their fascinating combination of a secluded subsistence farming lifestyle may be a characteristic that influenced their image. It is likely that it was due to the themes of literature in the works of their authors--as well as their affiliation with freemasons--they were recognized as a group who had various secrets and hidden ways. The historical cause of this could be the allegations of idol worship and unsavory ceremonies for initiation.

The Templars had been largely forgotten by the close of the 20th century, but were given renewed attention in Dan Brown's novel of the same name, The Da Vinci Code. The novel's fictional account of the Templars expanded some of the conspiracy theories previously presented and depicts The Order to have a hidden life , and hidden motives under the top of the.

Brown's story depicted the Templars as being in the Holy Land to liberate a cache of important documents which were believed to be found there, the documents of the Priory of Sion. While , in the time of the Templars (under their different names) they may have participated in various forms of treasure hunting, there is no evidence is available to support this fictional portrayal. Brown also depicted the Order as having the advantage of a secret that was eerie, and that they were more powerful, independent and rich than they actually were.

If you're looking for a mystery to solve, there's not one that isn't connected to the Templars and their hold on contemporary imaginations. The Templars were an elite police force that provided services to pilgrims who became great warriors. They had cool uniforms. They were scolded and were either forced to confess in mass to strange rituals they did not actually perform or participated in strange rituals. Then, they would go on the hunt for a mythical city full of treasure.

In our modern age there is a possibility that people of all ages are divided into two categories people who wish to protect others and those who wish to be secure.

Chapter 8: Pilgrimages, And The First Crusade

The Order of Poor Knights of the Temple of Solomon (the Knights Templar) was established in the second decade of the 12th century, with an extremely specific goal. Nobles pledged to defend Christian pilgrims who flocked to Jerusalem during the time that followed the First Crusade. The goal was to place the fledgling organisation within the rich historical background of religiously inspired travel. Saint Cletus Bishop from Rome who was also the third pope is believed to have instilled the belief that visiting the Relics from St. Peter and St. Paul is more beneficial to the salvation of the spirit than two consecutive years of fasting. The pope is a legend person who has no historical proof and the meaning behind the quotation is uncertain. The motivation behind it however, is real. A pilgrimage to holy places (Palestine specifically) to the purpose in visiting various shrines was made an element of Christian devotion at a very early stage despite the fact Christianity has never described this ritual as a requirement of all believers who could traveling - in contrast to the obligatory haj practiced in Islam.

In the course of spreading Christianity across the outskirts of the Roman empire, the holy sites in Palestine are the most sought-after location for many Christians were also the most distant. It is not known what percentage of faithful walked the risks of the long journey through the atmosphere of suspicion and hostility toward the new faith in the early years of Christianity. The first such pilgrimage with which we have reliable data is Melito of Sardis the bishop who traveled to Jerusalem as well as other places in Palestine in the year 170 A.D. (Eusebius, Hist. Eccl. 4.26.14). Other early pilgrims towards Jerusalem and the Holy Land were Clement of Alexandria (Stromata, 1.11.2), Origen and Pionius (Martyrium Pionii, 4,17). Journey to Jerusalem in the year 326-28, made by Helena who was the mother of Constantine, the Emperor Constantine is a significant event for the development of Christian pilgrimages.

...to the attention of the world The journey of Helena was highlighted by the same activities that are commonly associative with the journeys of any high-ranking official or grandee , such as the construction of structures and goodwill. But these had become channels to express the message of an Christian conviction that affected more deeply than conventions. When she made the transition from empress into pilgrim Helena eased the way for her successors. The travels of the pilgrims who sought out holy places were the norm in the Christian Roman empire (Hunt, 49).).

In a bid to emphasize the significance of the pilgrimage The Emperor's mother was able to conduct a search for significant relics. The search led to finding the "True Cross," the exact one that was believed to have been used in Jesus crucifying. With greater faith, Byzantine rulers built the Church of the Holy Sepulcher in the same spot where the relic was located and also built in Bethlehem the Church of Nativity in Bethlehem in order to visually affirm the elevated importance of these holy places. Their exact locations were established which made them "official" to the eyes of those who believe. With Christianity already being declared a national religion following the Edict of Milan (313) the foundations were put in place for a continuous flow of pilgrims, which hasn't been stopped, even in the face of numerous political and religious tensions in Palestine and the capital city of its past.

Some of the most difficult times for Western tourists visiting in the Holy Land, as well as Christians who resided there for a long time occurred during the time in which the area was completely in Muslim control. While Islamic doctrine emphasized acceptance of "People who are of the Bible," i. e. Jews and Christians, the actual behavior of people during various times were very different. Islamic rulers imposed a particular tax on non-Muslims that was meant to ensure that those of other religions could enjoy the protections of the Islamic-ruled state. However, the instability of the state and the constant threat of invading caused tensions between the religions in Jerusalem and in the towns around. Following a string of successful attacks by the Byzantine army at the beginning and 10th centuries the Muslims were able to take over a section of the outside court of the Church of the Holy Sepulcher. On Palm Sunday in 938, an Christian parade was attacked, and the Holy Sepulcher suffered some fire damage. In the days of Pentecost 966 churches were pillaged once further and John VII, Patriarch of Jerusalem was killed. Khaliph Hakim, who was particularly antagonistic towards Christians was the one who ordered the destruction of the Holy Sepulcher in 1009. In his diary of the time, reveals that the church was completely destroyed, and that attempts were made to degrade the actual sepulcher. He also reveals that Christians were required to change their religion to Islam and the majority of them did, with only a handful of people choosing to be martyred (perhaps as a sign of marginal conversions).

There is nothing that can stop Christian pilgrims from traveling to this Holy Land. The 11th century witnessed a dramatic increase in the number of pilgrims. The reasons for this varied. Western Europe was experiencing the time of economic recovery and the end of barbarian attacks. At that time it was believed that the Byzantine Empire was gaining control over the Eastern Mediterranean, allowing relatively secure journeys to Palestine. The desire to travel to the land where God's Word was made flesh was also driven by end-of-the-world expectations, since modern interpretations of biblical prophecies indicated that Christ's return to glory was coming soon. The precise timeframe for the coming end of the world was a bit different however many placed their faith on the importance of 1033 that marked a thousand years following Jesus died and rose again. In that year, massive crowds of pilgrims flocked by The Holy Land in hopes of witnessing the closing chapter of the human story. The so-called "Great German Pilgrimage of 1064 and 65" was also influenced by prophesies' interpretations, was a particular risky one. When the pilgrims finally arrived in Caesarea at the time of Good Thursday, 1065 , they believed that the risks of their journey at an end.

The following day Good Friday, which was on March 25. 1065], at 2 hours later [6.30-8 am], just as they left Kafar Sallam, they suddenly were seized by the Arabs who ran over them like hungry wolves in search of long-awaited prey. They massacred the first group of pilgrims in a cruel way by tearing them into pieces. Our people initially attempted to defend themselves, but were soon and forced, like poor people to flee the village. When they left and fled, who can describe the number of men who were killed as well as the various forms of deaths were there or how much destruction and pain was there? The bishop William of Utrecht severely wounded and stripped of clothes, lay on the ground along with others, and died a horrible end (Annalist of Nieder-Altaich in Serao 235-236).

The situation of Christian pilgrims to The Holy Land was not entirely due to ill-informed Muslim rulers. The instability of the region's politics and weak economic ties to the West caused the deficiency of infrastructure to support religious pilgrims. Food resources were in short supply and Westerners were exposed to a variety of illnesses that were mostly unknown to Westerners. In the final attempt of keeping out these visitors who were not welcome, Muslim authorities apparently forced people to pay for the right to enter into the Holy City:

When they entered the city, passing through hundreds of different types of death through the lands of enemies The city was closed to them , unless they had paid the gatekeepers at the Golden gate that was set for tolls. For those who had suffered a loss of everything in their journey and arrived at the destination barely alive, did not have anything to give as a payment. This meant that in the city, thousands or more were suffering from hunger and cold as they waited for the permission to be admitted (William from Tyre, Hist. Bell. Sacr. I, 10).

The stories of the suffering from Christians who were suffering in their Holy Land were heeded in the West with the greatest worry. It was evident that the land that was once blessed by Jesus himself was now hostile and dangerous for His faithful followers - whether visiting or living there for a long time. In the final years that of the 11th century,, there was a growing need to remedy the situation. The urgency that came with this mission is evident by the reality the Holy See of the Roman Catholic Church was able to resign from its recent stance of a bitter schism those of the Eastern Orthodox Church which was primarily led by the Patriarch from Constantinople. The long-running conflict over minor, to the modern eye issues of theology, worship practices, and the issue of supremacy of the pope was finally settled in 1054 with the mutual excommunications between pope Leo IX and the Patriarch of Constantinople. However, in 1095, when the pope Urban II began preaching about the First

Crusade, there was no denying that it was the case that most Christians who resided throughout the Holy Land and supposedly bearing the burden of Muslim attack were in fact Eastern Orthodox believers. In addition it was the demand from the Byzantine Emperor Alexius Comnenus I which served as a formal basis for the huge campaign. The emperor wanted assistance in the process of reclaiming Byzantine territories within Asia Minor from the Seljuk Turks and did not know the extent that would be the Western response which was to be followed.

The desire to assist fellow believers in remote area and the burning desire to ensure the right to holy sites weren't the only religious beliefs Urban II rely on. It was clearly stated to any Western Christian capable of embarking on a military journey into Jerusalem or the Holy Land that participation in this kind of campaign almost assured the salvation of all "whoever is devoted to God only, and not to obtain honor or wealth is able to go to Jerusalem to free God's Church God and then substitutes the trip for any sacrifices" (Canon 2, of the Council of Clermont).

The Crusades are often viewed as the most famous illustration of European imperialism. In the event that securing access for holy sites and offering assistance for Palestinian Christians could be seen as a sufficient reason to launch an expedition by force but there are other factors to be considered. Al-Arabi is a renowned Andalusian Muslim, has that of Palestine: "The country is theirs (the Christiansas it is the Christians who manage the soil, tend to the monasteries of its abbeys and manage the churches of its people" (Gil 1992 171.) This was written on the eve of First Crusade, because al-Arabi resided in Jerusalem between 1093 and 1095. It is often not understood that Christians were living in Palestine for a long time, from the very beginning times of Christianity. They were never being considered a minority, regardless of the fact that Muslim invaders took over across the country, and imposed an incredibly high tax on "infidels" and occasionally turning to violence. The existence in Palestine before the First Crusades depended on its Christian population not the elite and warrior classes of various Muslim groups who fought for control over the region. To claim that the Crusades were attempts to claim Palestine as a place of

Christianity isn't true especially when you consider the ferocious territorial expansion of Islam in the preceding centuries.

The first call to arms was issued through Pope Urban II at the council of Clermont on the 27th of November 1095. The sermon of the supreme Pontiff could be received with more enthusiasm. Everyone who agreed to participate in the mission could be identified by their appearance. It was Abbot Guibert of Jerusalem in the History of Jerusalem says that Pope Urban II ordained the idea that a cross be used as a symbol of military distinction as well as an emblem that could help Christian knights to fight with greater determination for the cause of God. The abbot explains that the pope commanded the cross's figure to be removed from any material (ex cujuslibet material) and sewn onto the cloaks and tunics of those who were part from the group. The terms we use in the present to describe this period (Crusades or crusaders) are not new and are an evocation of the spirit of the movement and the significance to use the Cross as a symbol. Fulcher from Chartres said: "How fitting and how delightful it was for us all to look at those crosses, embroidered in gold or silk, or constructed from any material that the Pilgrims on the orders of the Pope made onto their shoulders after vowing to begin this journey!"

The First Crusade consisted of two major waves. The paupers Crusade led by the Walter Sans Avoir (the Penniless) and Peter the Hermit created a lot of trouble in its journey toward Asia Minor where this massive inexperienced and unorganized group was destroyed by the Seljuks in the month of October 1096. It was the Princes' Crusade that was more prepared, and following two years of battle in the region, they had captured Nicaea, Caeserea, Dorylaeum and Antioch The Christian forces took over Jerusalem in the month of June 1099. Jerusalem fell on the 15th of July. The Jerusalem's Eastern Orthodox population had been removed because of fears that they would aid the Crusaders. According to current Western information, exuberant triumphant soldiers indiscriminately killed all who were still within the city's walls. But, Muslim sources from the also at that time do not confirm the horrific massacre which took place at Temple Mount "men rode in blood until their knees" according to what Raymond from Aguilers (an eyewitness) would like us to believe.

The region was split into various areas that were to function much the same way as independent realms of Western Europe. The time of Crusader states in the Holy Land began.

The Order of the Knights Templar

The beginning of the year

While it was true that the First Crusade was by no any means a typical trip, the participants shared a commonality with the thousands of pilgrims who had travelled to Jerusalem earlier. After a few days exploring Jerusalem, Holy Land they were ready to return back to their homes. Since their predecessors, the Latin Christians established the sovereign Kingdom of Jerusalem together with a variety of counties and principalities Their presence as a military in the Levant decreased. Without any police on the roads and routes, the most well-known routes utilized by pilgrims turned treacherous. Travelers were constantly at risk of being robbed or killed by brigands belonging to various groups. The creation of the Order of the Knights Templar was precisely the radical new kind of commitment required for this part of the Holy Land.

The earliest records of the founding and development of this Order have been extremely scarce. The three earliest chroniclers considered trustworthy sources for the subject are William of Tyre (d. 1186), Michael the Syrian (d. 1199) and Walter Map (died between 1208 and 1210) (Barber 1994 6). The story told in these sources is that, at around the middle in the middle of the 12th century's second decade (1118 A.D. is the most likely date) nine knights of noble blood took a vow to serve God by defending pilgrims from bandits and thieves. They decided to take vows of chastity, poverty, and obedience, in the style that was practiced by Canons Regular - clerics living in a fraternal society. Canons Regular typically participated in public service, but without becoming monks. They were also involved in public ministry. Church of the Holy Sepulcher in Jerusalem was home to one of these fraternities and even the early Templars were believed to be a part of the church. This type of spiritual discipline suggested that knights had to follow the Augustinian rules (followed by certain monastic instructions) however instead of living the contemplative and liturgical lifestyle like normal monks, they would carry arms and stand in defence for their Christian fight in Palestine. A Patriarch from Jerusalem the highest spiritual authorities in the world of Catholics within Crusader States, was naturally selected as the spiritual head for the newly established order to whom they pledged their loyalty.

It seems that the knights could quickly win approval from civil officials. King Baldwin II gave them partial access to the Al-Aqsa mosque, which was located in the Temple Mount. The building, dubbed "The Temple of Solomon" by the Crusaders served as a palace for the royals and, without doubt, was a desirable piece of property. It served as the base for the new band of religious nobles, who later began declaring themselves as the Knights of the Temple of Solomon or the Poor Knights of Christ (indicating their pledge of personal poorness). The Crusaders might not have had any understanding of their knowledge of the Old Testament and ancient history however, they likely knew extremely well about the Al-Aqsa mosque, which was originally built in the 8th century by

Umayyads around the time of the 8th century wasn't the real Temple of Solomon. But the significance of the place and possibly the notion that the building was situated on an old foundation made the name "Temple of Solomon" possible. It is important to remember that the most impressive structure in Jerusalem is the Dome of the Rock, frequently believed as the site of Solomon's Temple was known during the Crusaders times in the Crusaders' time as being known to be"the Temple of the Lord. This is likely due to the fact that it was believed to be the spot in which Jesus was seen and spoke at Herod's Temple. It is believed that the Dome of the Rock was constructed in the year 691 A.D. with assistance from Byzantine architects. In many ways it is reminiscent of it's counterpart, the Church of the Holy Sepulcher. The domed structure visible on some Knights Templar seals can be identified as either the Dome of the Rock or the Church of the Holy Sepulcher as neither has its medieval look today. It is probable that it was the initial Temple of Solomon is symbolically depicted in the seal's design, which was inspired by the most famous houses that were used for worship within Jerusalem during the time.

The creation of an devoted Christian group tasked with specific responsibilities is not a new phenomenon. A semi-monastic organization called the Hospitallers existed established since the year 1080 A.D., overseeing medical services and sheltering facilities for pilgrims. The organization was set to evolve into a full-fledged military order, however at the time they became the Knights Templar became incorporated the Hospitallers did not have such ambitions. There is evidence that the Templars received help from the Hospitallers in their first few years of existence (Barber 1994, 8,).

Two French noblemen from France, Hugues de Payens of Champagne as well as Godfrey de St Omer from Picardy was the primary person responsible for the formation of Knights Templar, and the total number of knights who took on the three vows of monastic piety was just nine. A few of the initial Templars are recognized as their real names: Payen de Montdidier, Andre de Montbard, Archambaud de Saint Aignan as well as Geoffroi Bisol. Two knights are known through the Christian name: Roland and Gondemar. Name of ninth charter member is in the dark (Martin Martin, 25). This one incident could be a clue to the possibility that the initial order was not exactly the believed to be auspicious number nine. The same numerological logic could be the reason for the fact that, as per the traditions, the early Knights Templar displayed no growth within their ranks over the entirety of the initial decade of their existence.

According to an alternative theory, the initial group of Templars simply did not have a desire in sharing the various secrets they were discovering in the midst of their ability to access temples on the Temple Mount. If learning to keep secrets rather than protecting pilgrims were the Templars' primary goal then why would they need to intensify their efforts in recruiting? There exist numerous underground tunnels, cisterns, and other structures that can be accessed directly from the Templars headquarters. Archaeological evidence proves that the Knights were indeed attempting to investigate these old spaces and it's difficult to establish that if there was anything there the Templars were not able to make fascinating discoveries. In addition it is not amazed that the membership roster for the newly founded order was not as full for a period of time. The main issue they attempted to tackle was the lack of knights within Palestine. Of of course, a hundred knights would have been more effective in securing religious pilgrims in their journey to the Holy Land, but even nine men with armed guards could be the distinction between life or death for thousands of pilgrims, making the robbery of highways into a more dangerous business. One of the biggest challenges the first Templars faced was the inability to connect to resources of the West (both physical as well as financial). This made the exponential expansion within the Order impossible. But they Knights Templar must have shown the potential and their early efforts were rewarded soon enough.

In the latter part of 1127 the Grand Master who was the first to be elected of the Knights Templar, Hugues de Payens was on a trip to Europe together with other royal officials who were tasked to ensure that the army was constantly reinforced from the West and to seek a solution for the imminent dynastic crisis that was threatening Jerusalem.

Jerusalem. The old Baldwin II didn't have an heir of males. The Baldwin II was obliged to search for a successor after the marriage of his most senior daughter, Melisende. Both the goals of this significant mission were finally fulfilled. Fulk V., the Count of Anjou was willing for a trip to Jerusalem and be a part of Baldwin's daughter on her wedding day, however, there were some issues with the diplomatic side that had to be resolved to ensure the success of the union. The achievement in de Payens' efforts, however was unqualified and complete. He was the Grand Master of Knights Templar was able to personally announce the existence of the Order to Scotland and huge contributions of land and cash quickly began flooding into. For many people with wealth, it was a great idea to fund the knights that could take on the infidels as well as offer prayer for the spirits of Order's patrons and their family members.

The only thing to be done was ensure they Knights Templar were within the structure within the Catholic church. To achieve this goal, Hugues de Payens found an extremely powerful ally in Bernard de Clairvaux (1090 - 1153) A popular preacher and reformer from the Cistercian Order. The charismatic abbot had connections to his fellow Knights Templar. Bernard had acquired the property to build his monastic establishment in Clairvaux by Hugues, the Count of Champagne and had as one of the vassals of his Hugues de Payens. More interestingly the family tree of Bernard's maternal uncle is believed to be Andre de Montbard, one of the founding nine participants of the Knights Templar. The abbot was well-informed about the struggles and needs for members of the Knights who lived in Outremer (French word meaning "the overseas land"). Bernard de Clairvaux even reportedly wrote the very first Rule for the Knights Templar (known as the Latin Rule), outlining the basic principles that governed the Order's founding. He also was instrumental in the organization of an annual regional council in Troyes in 1129. It authorized the Knights Templar, with Pope Honorius II giving his personal approval.

Nearly two decades before the events of this era in the past, the Hospitallers were going through the same process of getting papal approval. The establishment of the Knights Templar however, had a totally distinct character. The new order wasn't intended to be a normal monastic establishment. In all practical terms the monks were permitted to kill - something that many familiar with Catholic theology had a difficult to accept. Though pacifist voices won't be absent from Christian discussions however, the issue needed to be addressed with Bernard de Clairvaux himself. In a fiery pamphlet "In The Name of the New Knighthood" he emphasized that the murder of criminals shouldn't be considered murder. Bernard transformed what many believed to be the Templars weaknesses, such as the dual nature of their status as monks and soldiers in their power. They were the New Knighthood was urged to take on all forces of evil, both in the spirit as well as in the flesh.

Overall it is evident that the founding Of the Order of St. John was positively accepted in Western Europe, as evidenced by the donations of money and land that grew in popularity in the 12th century's middle. Numerous wills and charters from the period of time show that offering aid to the Temple is a high priority in the hierarchy of giving to religious institutions and that those who prayed for the Poor Knights of Christ were believed to be effective for the wellbeing and the salvation of their donors.

In 1139 the aid which was initially provided in 1139 to Knights Templar by the Holy See was significantly strengthened through the Holy See's special decree. The official declarations issued by the Pope are called bulls, named for the seal of lead (bulla) which is associated with the documents. According to the tradition, these documents get titles that are based on biblical passages that are usually quoted in the first lines of every bull. This bull was crucially important in establishing the authority that was the Knights Templar is called Omne Datum. The phrase that translates to "Every good present" is derived directly from the Epistle of James: "Every best and perfect gift comes from above, and comes directly from God, the father of the heavenly light, who is not influenced by moving shadows" (James 1:17 New International Version). The bull established policies that govern the Knights Templar place in the Catholic church. It was also the case that Knights Templar were proclaimed to not be taxed by either church or civil authorities. They were able to make use of the spoils of war and also donations from their patrons to meet their obligations and needs. The independence in the realm of spirituality was achieved through giving members of the Knights Templar to have their own priests and churches - which was a necessity given the challenging conditions in which the Order was operating in remote regions. The fact that they had their own priests assisted to allow the Knights Templar to fulfill their obligation to the donors who desired that their name be honored in celebrations of the Mass. The most important thing is that the bull stated that Knights Templar from now on were an autonomous entity that was accountable exclusively to Pope himself. This status of jurisdiction continued to be in force throughout the entire period of the Order's history up to the Templars fell in 1307 when the power of the Pope was publicly contest through the King of France.

Omne Datum Optimum that was released by the Pope Innocent II, as well as the subsequent decrees passed from the successors of Celestine II as well as Eugene III, created conditions that allowed for the rapid expansion in the Knights Templar. Military orders were deemed as the best tool for maintaining control over in the Holy Land. The Templars originally had the task to protect Christian pilgrims could be supported by their actions in Europe which saw the resources required for the East were gathered and then moved to Palestine. A standing army could be provided with support by Outremer and the costs of constructing and maintaining castles would be able to be paid for. In the midst of this project is strict discipline and devotion of the rank and filial participants from the Knights Templar Order, organized by the principles outlined in the known as Latin Rule.

Discipline and organization

Like other medieval institutions Like all institutions of the medieval period, like all medieval institutions, the Order of the Knights Templar was a feudal institution and had a clearly defined order of things. The most prestigious position of the Order is Master (modern writers only use the word Grand Master, and it will be utilized in this book as well). He was the headquarter of Jerusalem (and afterwards at Acre as well as Cyprus) the Master performed the highest administrative and disciplinary duties. A council 12 senior brother (the amount of Jesus' first Apostles) was a part of the Grand Master's team. In making major decisions, like membership of the Order or other important financial and business issues as well as other business and financial matters, it was the Templar Rule dictated the Grand Master to convene a meeting with the Council. The council also had the duty of the council to choose one of the leaders following the death of the Grand Master. The post of Grand Master was a lifetime commitment. There was only one Grand Master. Philip de Milly, left his position in order to go back to the secular world. Evrard des Barres after being the Templar Grand Master ultimately left and was accepted into in the Cistercian Order in the year 1151 (Nicholson 114). Templar Statutes clearly state that the members of the Order were required to pledge their allegiance to the Grandmaster who had several exclusive rights in the sense of governing the lives of officers and knights. The Grand Master was a target of retribution. were considered serious. For instance lying to him may cause him to be expelled from the Order. The authority and responsibility of being a Grandmaster is described as follows: "All the brothers of the Temple must follow the Master's instructions, and the Master must obey his home" (Upton-Ward 44).

While not explicitly mentioned in the initial Templar Rule, several additional important positions were in place within the Order. Seneschals were the Grand Master's deputy as well as personal advisor. A marshal was in charge of the military's decisions, in addition to anything that was related to horses and weapons. They also had to deal with horses and weapons. Knights Templar were uniformly clothed they were the duty of the drapers to ensure that appropriate clothes were given to brothers, and that the Templar "dress dress code" was adhered to. Provincial masters, accountable before the Grandmaster were in charge of managing the activities of the Order within their respective regions: France, England, Aragon, Poitou, Portugal, Apulia and Hungary (Haag 2009, 130). Turcopoliers served as the commanding officers of local light cavalry units that were auxiliary to the. The commanding officers had full power over subordinate officers charged with various tasks.

Most well-known and respected, naturally was the knights. The noble members of Europe's families would have received a high-quality military training prior to entering the Order. After leaving the lifestyles typical of their age They made vows of chastity sacrifice and obedience, as well as being prepared to serve in extremely harsh conditions (the Order was typically stationed with only a few knights in regions in which there were no active combat operations). In being a servant of God and even committing to the cross to honor His name, they were determined to secure their salvation, and also to further advance to advance the cause of Christianity within Outremer. It was their right of wearing white mantles representing purity, and the red cross to symbolize their choice of a martyr's path. Knights were required to be well-equipped, and were permitted to have squires out of necessity. For military purposes the second most significant function within the Knights Templar Order was that of sergeants. Sergeants were also well-trained warriors, who, despite being part of the order, didn't swear monastic vows. Instead of white mantles given to knight-brothers' sergeants, sergeant-brothers black or , sometimes, dark brown mantles with red crosses. The color of the crosses on their uniforms was a way to distinguish them from Knights Hospitaller, who wore black mantles and white crosses. There was also a tradition of European nobles of joining to the Knights Templar for a short time. Similar to sergeants, sergeants were not permitted to wear white robes. In addition, one could be a part of the Order with the special position of a confrerere. Associate members usually left an inheritance of a significant amount to the Order as well as afiliating their families with the Templars. Apart from people belonging to the Knights Templar who were actively involved in war There were other tasks that were crucial to the success of the Order, including craftsmen grooms, masons and clerks. A few among the Knights Templar commanderies in the West were little more than agricultural structures that were modestly constructed and staffed to serve as an income source for the operation of the Order in Outremer.

For more than two centuries, millions of people remained strictly observing the Templar Rule (despite the fact that not all could comprehend the rule on Latin). Their lives were governed by the same spiritual rules as those of a monastic order. Each member was expected to attend multiple service times a day, and substitute for them individual prayers when events in the military rendered regular services unaffordable. The emphasis of the Templars on their spirituality is explained in a medieval tale about a knights' group who were aware of the imminent attack of the enemy when they were praying at their church. The Templars were instructed by their superiors to continue praying and managed to conclude their prayers without disturbance. After the knights had dispersed from their worship, they found out that a war was just taking place outside the church and all their foes were killed. It was evident that angels were pleased with the sight of knights worshiping fighting in their place (Nicholson 141). A moral code for Knights Templar was one of the most strict during the Middle Ages. They were required to refrain from the indulgences that were typical for the warriors at the day. There was no tolerance for drinking, gambling, swearing or sexual activity in any form. Hunting was also not allowed to people of the Order, as it was an act of entertainment. It seems it was the Knights Templar had more success as per their vows than other monks (Nicholson 140).

The guidelines to military maneuvers, tactics along with battle-formations, were described as part of the Templar Rule. When a command was issued by the commander, it was expected that the Knights Templar were required to lead the way to join an engagement and the last to withdraw. They were required to fight, even if their regiments dispersed and the Order's flag was taken by enemy forces and in that case, it was their responsibility to go to the closest Christian banner in place on the battleground. Together with the strict discipline they enforced and instructions, to allow the Knights Templar to be the most revered Christian army in Outremer. As they entered battle, they Templars would respond to the sound of the drum, singing the Psalm with the Order's famous motto, "Non Nobis Domine, non nobis Domine, sed Nomini Tuo da glory (Not to us, Lord, not to us and to the name of Thy Name glorify). This battle hymn was usually followed by a massive cavalry battle, which was the most spectacular show of force that was seen in the Middle Ages. If captured Templars were frequently executed due to the fact that their Muslim adversaries did not view the ransom as a valid reason for them to stand up against them again one day.

Medieval military strategies relied heavily on the construction of formidable strongholds in crucial areas. Orders from the military directed huge sums of money to build and maintaining castles. Some of the most important fortresses managed by Knights Templar included Baghras, Gaza, Acre, La Feve and Tortosa. The importance of castles for defense of Outremer required the most recent advancements in military technology and architecture. Atlit Castle, also known as Atlit Castle, also called Castle Pilgrim (in the honor of Christians travelers who worked to build it) is a great illustration of the Templars construction program. The fortress that was built located south of Haifa could hold up to 4,000 soldiers in a siege. The Knights Templar generally didn't build Fortified fortresses in Western Europe. However, their participation of the

Reconquista ("reconquest") of the Iberian peninsula demanded strategies that were like those employed in Outremer. The final success of these efforts to bring present current Spain as well as Portugal back to the tradition of Christianity was partly due to castles constructed that were maintained and maintained with the help of members of the Knights Templar: Almourol, Calatrava, Toledo, Tomar, Soure and many others.

Templars have wealth

In a sense, almost out of necessity, Knights Templar quickly assumed another crucial role in bridging both the West with the East as the world's most prestigious financial institution. The houses of the religious have been utilized to store valuables as well as important documents since through the Middle Ages. They were the Knights Templar were able to take advantage of this tradition by using the trust that they earned in their authority and honesty. As a global organisation and a global organization, the Order was the first to provide global financial assistance. The necessity of transferring the funds of Europe to

Outremer was fulfilled through the credit note system. One could deposit money at the Knights Templar residence in the West and receive an encrypted note that can be exchanged in return for deposit at a different branch located in Levant or anywhere else (Haag 140-141). The credit notes were not of inherent value, which made the robbery and theft less feasible - yet another way that the Templars were able to fulfill their original role to protect pilgrims, although in indirect ways. The constant dealings with huge amounts of money boosted the Knights Templar's expertise in matters of financial shrewdness. They kept track of each transaction by using a debit-credit system for accounting. Their customers received regular reports. Since they were Knights Templar were treated very well in the eyes of the Holy See as a result of their financial services also included lending - a practice which was forbidden by the Catholic Church to Christians at the time. Since the Templars were not subject to taxes, their operating expenses were low while interest charges could be seen in loans, which were portrayed as penalty or service charges. The Order was able to provide large sums of money from the beginning of 1148 which was when the Templars together with the Hospitallers created an urgent money loan for Louis VII, the King Louis VII of France during the Second Crusade. The relationship to the French monarchy was to the point that the Templars have a strength in Paris effectively was transformed into the royal Treasury. The massive compound, also known by the name of Paris Temple, originally built around 1146, was a visual representation of the power and prestige of the Order. Its counterpart, the London Temple, of which only one chapel remains, should be comparable in size and style. While it was true that the Knights Templar headquarters in England was not at the status of the royal treasury, the those who were members were frequently hired in the hands of English monarchs in crucial post of advisory and diplomatic positions.

The Knights Templar were quite opportunistic in seeking out new sources of revenue which led to a growing problem when charitable donations began to decrease during the middle of the thirteenth century. Based on the local climate, Templar commanderies operated agricultural and sheep farms grain mills, forges, grain mills and wineries, breweries and also participated in building projects. In Castle Pilgrim Castle Pilgrim, the Knights Templar had a salting facility. They also pursued advanced types of industrial activities such as the extraction of coal, metal ores, the production of cloth as well as glass, smelting, and smelting. They were usually located in peaceful regions and didn't require any military security (Nicholson, 1887).

Always dependent on the supply of The West In the past, Knights Templar found themselves in the business of importing horses crops, coins, and iron out of Europe into Outremer. They also provided travelers with an opportunity to travel across Outremer, the Holy Land and back under the security of the Order's armoured men. In the beginning, they Knights Templar did not have their own fleet, and relied heavily upon chartering ships to fulfill their requirements. The 13th century saw this changed as the Order aimed to reach the objective of becoming independent on the seas. This was noticeable in Templars in their efforts to purchase the vessels of their own for commercial use. In the same period it was evident that the Knights Hospitaller were beginning to recognize that the significance of naval combat. This trend was likely to continue, since the hospital's military history following it had been through the Crusades during the Holy Land revolved around sea-based campaigns. It is certain that, if it was the case that Order of the Knights Templar was able to continue for a long time, its existence would have also depended from naval battles. However, it is unlikely that by the end of the Order's existence, the Templars could begin explorations in oceans like the Atlantic Ocean, as believed by some contemporary Templar supporters. Particularly, these ships could not hold enough fresh water or food for long-distance journeys, and were better equipped to navigate the low-lying Mediterranean Sea where everything necessary was easily accessible from the coast.

The riches that was the property of Knights Templar was considerable. However, significant portions of it was held in non-monetary forms and therefore could not be transformed into currency. These included property ownership rights, land outstanding contracts, loans equipment, and other goods that had short shelf lives. The worth of the Templars company was the way in which they were able to manage all of these assets and ensure that the objective of keeping this Holy Land in Christian hands was never out of reach for all who was involved. Things that transpired in Outremer in the latter half in the thirteenth century rendered the goals less attainable The dissolution of the Order resulted in a loss of central power , which was required to sustain and modernize the vast economy. While a lot of the Templars owned possessions were transferred from their Pope and their fellow Knights Hospitaller, the Templars' wealth was not transferable, and their entire financial and economic empire ended to exist in its entirety. Therefore, the existence of any Templar treasure is in doubt. There is evidence that suggests an entire flotilla Templar ships that left La Rochelle port. La Rochelle soon after the notorious arrests that were conducted across France. There is no further information on the ships has been discovered. One could speculate that the fleet carried an abundance of coins or rare metals (or even precious relics from Temple of the Sun). Temple). It is equally simple to conclude that the vessel was transporting wine that was produced by Templar wineries close to La Rochelle, known for exporting the fruits of their vineyards via ship (Nicholson, the year 192).

Chapter 9: Campaigning In Outremer

As far as the Templars were concerned, the diverse roles they took on always had one primary objective - to oversight on all of the Holy Land, keeping it secure for pilgrims and Christian residents. Although the majority of the activities of the Order particularly in the West was not based on the use of weapons but it was the Knights Templars' troops were crucial in Outremer. As one might expect, they actively participated in war campaigns led through the Catholic Church as well as European monarchs.

In the Second Crusade (1147-1149) the Knights Templar were already showing they had superior discipline, as well as understanding. It is the very first significant military operation of the West following the successful retake from Jerusalem along with in the Holy Land at the end of the 11th century. Christian state in Palestine were enjoying a prolonged period of peace and stability until the time they were occupied by a Seljuk Turk by the name of Imad Ad-Din

Zengi seized the county with no land Edessa in 1144 along with his army. It took a few years to wait for the West to react by deploying full force. Bernard de Clairvaux, the charismatic abbot who was who was responsible for the rapid growth of Knights Templar was instrumental in energizing European Christians for this new cause. The Crusade however, was hit with initial setbacks that it ultimately failed to overcome. The German army was led by Conrad III, was attacked by Seljuk Turks on its march through Asia Minor and was forced to retreat to Constantinople. It was the French force under leadership by Louis VII also suffered heavy losses while traversing the Cadmus mountains. The light Seljuk cavalry could easily target knights with guns with archers. Everard de Barres, the head of the Knights Templar in France was able to save Louis the army by breaking the troops into smaller groups which were each controlled by the Templar. Even though the troops were eventually brought to safety on the Mediterranean coast close to Attalia it was made impossible. The Byzantine fleet was unable to transport every single one of the French to Palestine in the manner anticipated, so a huge group in Louis' army tried to make it to their destination continuing to march across enemy territory, an approach that was fatal. After the final defeat of all Christian forces, which included Conrad with the remaining part of his army and Louis VII with his much weaker French troops, the original objective of capturing Edessa was completely impossible. The alternative was Damascus is the preferred target in this unfortunate campaign despite the fact that the city was run by an administration which had previously expressed an interest in joining forces to those in the West in the fight against Zengi (who passed away on the year 1146) along with his son Nur al-Din. The Christian army landed at Damascus however, they failed to erect an effective siege, and they retreated in July 1148. The ensuing finger-pointing ensued, it was claimed that the Knights Templar were accused of being the ones to blame for the defeat after having accepted the offer of bribe (according some myths that, after they were greedy Templars have opened the funds in the coffers, the bribes they took from Damascus proved to be insignificant). The charge, though insignificant by the majority of reports, was likely to make sense to Conrad and the other newcomers to in the Holy Land who mistook the Templars their ability to negotiate between rival Islamic factions for treachery or corruption. While it was true that the Second Crusade, was overwhelmingly unsuccessful, a lot of the Templars tactics for military were successful and the Order certainly improved its image regardless of allegations they were accused of.

In 1177, the Knights Templar participated in a triumphant battle of Christian troops against Saladin in Montgisard. The Egyptian sultan proved an imposing opponent, and he fought in a devastating victory over the Crusaders in Hattin in 1187 that left the Holy Land virtually defenseless. Following the defeat the Saladin imposed to surrender Jerusalem following an ensuing siege, on terms that permitted the safe passage of Christians who were looking to leave the city in the event that ransom was paid. The destruction of Jerusalem directly triggered an outbreak of the Third Crusade, confirming the strategy that worked throughout the rest of the West's military activities in Outremer and elsewhere: defeat was greeted with greater enthusiasm. This effort, which was a joint effort between Philip II's French troops from Philip II and the English army under the command of Richard I, known by the name "the Lionheart" proved to be one of the most prosperous Christian campaign throughout the Holy Land. Richard I was adamant about not taking on Jerusalem following the advice of The Knights Templar, as well the Hospitallers of the time, that the city could be difficult to control in the event of its capture. But, as per the treaty signed by the Muslims, Jerusalem became once again open to Christians Pilgrims. Despite the shrinking size of the Latin states, the Western participation in Outremer continued to be strong and enduring. The Knights Templar, who played crucial in the Third Crusade, were able to set up the new home of their headquarters at Acre which was recently captured and heavily fortified city located on the Mediterranean coast of Palestine.

The period that followed after the Third Crusade could have been utilized to improve the Christians standing in Outremer. However, certain goals that were pursued through the Holy See (and the West generally) in the early part in the thirteenth century were found to be harmful to the cause that they were Knights Templar stood throughout their existence. The known as Fourth Crusade began as a noble undertaking, fuelled by the lackluster outcomes that were a result of the Third Crusade. In the meantime, the Holy Sepulcher remained in the control of the Muslims and the notion of acquiring Jerusalem completely and forever was taking hold within the hearts of a lot of devout Catholics. In the year 1202 the Crusade comprised of mostly French as well as Flemish knights was set to embark to in the East from Venice and the local shipyards were responsible for the construction of huge fleets of transport ships and galleys. In the end, having fulfilled their portion of the agreement however, the Venetians did not permit the beginning of the Crusade until they were compensated to compensate them for the effort. A deal was struck that the Crusaders were to pay off their debts by first attacking some Byzantine ports. The Byzantine Empire was for a long time Venice's biggest adversary in the Mediterranean and the two sea-faring powerhouses were at a particular bad time in their relationship.

In the late November of 1202 The dispersed Crusading army occupied and seized Zara, a city Zara in the Dalmatian coast. After bringing this port into Venetian rule and re-established it as a Venetian port, the Crusaders chose to remain there until the duration of winter. Due to the financial difficulties that plagued the venture right from the beginning It was hard to resist the urge to interfer with Byzantium's internal political affairs whenever the chance presented itself. The members of the Fourth Crusade took the side of Alexios IV Angelos, eager to restore to the Imperial Kingship to the father of his children by removing the usurper, his paternal uncle Alexios III Angelos. Exiled Byzantine prince offered military and financial assistance in exchange for assistance. After numerous assaults, Constantinople was finally captured by the Crusaders in the month of April of 1204. The subsequent turmoil led to the weakening of the Byzantine Empire, which was ruled by the Western dynasty. Pope Innocent III attempted to leverage this outcome that was not expected from the Fourth Crusade to bring Byzantium under the full supervision by the Roman Catholic Church. At this time where those who were the Knights Templar along with the Knights Hospitaller were told to send their own troops to Byzantine areas, far away to their native Holy Land.

The Latin kingdom of Constantinople lasts for over a half century, and resulted in a drain on Western resources that could have been utilized for Outremer. There was a presence in the Knights Templar within Byzantium was not without its own facets. It is at the margins of the field of study in historical research however, with time it will be more widely accepted. It is believed that the Templars were the owners of the relic that over a century later came back to life to be known as the Shroud of Turin. The massive looting of ancient artifacts and relics which occurred following the occupation of Constantinople in fact brought a flood of precious objects returning towards the West. The relic, dubbed the Mandylion and is believed to be an unimaginably beautiful towel imprinted with the image of Jesus Christ, may have actually been the supposed burial shroud which has puzzled researchers and enthralled believers for a long time. It was folded in order to conceal the face of Christ's entire body and to conceal the image of Jesus Christ, the Mandylion was utilized for Imperial ceremonies and later as a secret symbol of Templar ceremonies. This is backed with the knowledge that the Shroud of Turin made its debut in the middle of the 14th century, it was owned by a man named Geoffroi de Charny. He was most likely an ancestor of his name's full ancestor (with the only exception of a different spelling of his last name) A high-level Templar who was burned at the stake and Jacques de Molay in 1314 (see Barbara Frale's book "The Templars and the Shroud of Christ").

Another issue that the Papacy faced at the early thirteenth century was the spreading of Catharism, particularly in present-day Southern France. This heretical group of sectarian Christians which believed God or Satan were equally powerful power was resisted through the Catholic Church, using every option to be used. The fight with the Cathars came to be known by the name of Albigensian Crusade which lasted for several decades. In the end, Knights Templar did not participate in military attacks on the Cathars. However, this conflict was against the goal of ensuring the stability of Outremer.

In 1217 in 1217, the Papacy came back towards the notion of taking back Jerusalem. The troops at the Vatican's to be used were mostly German as well as Hungarian knights, while France was in the midst of its involvement in the Albigensian Crusade. Military orders in Outremer consistently supplied the majority troops from their soldiers however, the lack of soldiers was evident shortly thereafter. The Crusade was initially successful in taking Damietta which was a major Egyptian port. There, the Knights Templar were able to win the day with the help of ships and pontoons. the Sultan of Egypt, Al-Kamil (Saladin's nephew) was so enraged that offered Jerusalem as a trade-off for strategically important Damietta. The offer was turned down due to the fact that Jerusalem was not considered to be safe without control over the surrounding regions. But the campaign stagnated waiting for its arrival Frederick II, the Holy Roman Emperor who was to be a part of the Crusade. The Sultan employed new warfare strategies, including opening the sluices in irrigation canals, while the Christians began to march toward Cairo. The Crusaders' troops became unorganized and easily defeated. The first gains made by the Fifth Crusade were quickly reverted.

Frederick II was finally able to fulfill by fulfilling his pledges in 1228. The well-educated and eccentric ruler of Christendom is believed to have held the philosophical and religious views of his time out of the traditional Catholic religion, was mostly focused on personal gain. Nothing could have added to his title list more than the crowning of as King of Jerusalem. The chance to do that was presented by the marriage of Yolanda her daughter Jean de Brienne, King of Jerusalem and the ruler of the Latin Empire of Constantinople. A shrewd leader for the Sixth Crusade, Frederick II technically was not even able to cross the cross after being disproved in the Vatican by pope Gregory IX for the failure to appear in Damietta. This also led to him being be snubbed and even hated by the majority of Christians within Outremer. He was not able to win the approval of the military and, in the end, only those of the Teutonic Knights. Through smart diplomacy, Holy Roman Emperor negotiated the return of Jerusalem under the control of Crusading forces after agreeing to terms that did not mean anything to the individual. The truce only lasted for a period of ten years. Only a small portion of land was granted in order to link Jerusalem and other Latin landmasses in Palestine and it was the Temple Mount remained in the control of Muslims. It was the case that the patriarch of Jerusalem had banned worship services for the church in Jerusalem when the Emperor was in the city and so Frederick II crowned himself at the Church of the Holy Sepulcher on the 29th of March, 1229. He quit in the Holy Land soon after, having accomplished his goals.

In 1244, a few times after the peace treaty ended, Jerusalem was lost to the Mamelukes, the clan comprised of Egyptian military slaves who managed to gain prominence as an entirely Muslim faction. In the month of October that same the year Christian troops suffered a brutal defeat in the vicinity of a location called La Forbie. Nearly 300 Knights Templar were killed, which makes it the most brutal fight since Hattin. The Crusaders lost around 5 000 men in total. It was the Seventh Crusade, led by King Louis IX of France, was launched a few years later. Participation by French nobility was feasible, as the Cathars had finally been dispersed by the time of the crusade (the crucial battle of Montsegur the last significant stronghold of the Cathars ended a few months prior to the surrender of Jerusalem in 1244). The crusade failed but it was a failure, and the Knights Templar lost another 280 knights mounted at the time of the war of Mansurah.

From then on, the enthusiasm level for issues in Outremer within European Christians began to steadily decrease, as the odds weren't in the Crusaders favour. Their Muslim adversaries continued to increase their maneuvering skills and siege of castles, and were adept at leveraging enormous human and financial resources from nearby lands. The cost of keeping Christian governments within the East was increasing as support for the state in the West was decreasing. It was the Knights Templar and the Knights Hospitaller did not lose their resolve to maintain their steadfast position in the East However, their Crusader kingdoms began declining in size and their savability. The fall to Acre in 1291 was the final blow to Christian forces of Outremer.

Headquarters of the Knights Templar were relocated again in 1291, but this time in 1291, to Cyprus.

The Templars and the Hospitallers were blamed for the events that occurred in Palestine Some voices within the Church were even advocating that military orders be merged into one. It was the grand master of the Knights Templar, Jacques de Molay who was elected in 1292, vehemently insisted on the necessity of keeping his order, however to the eyes of many, they believed that it was no longer serving a purpose. As Templar leadership was concerned about plans to make another attempt to recapture their claim to the Holy Land, the situation was transformed from one of uncertainty into one that was completely catastrophic.

The collapse of the Order

The events at the start thirteenth century which led to the dissolution of the Knights Templar had a complex background. The famous Templar trials clearly demonstrate the decline of papal power as the new nation-states of Western Europe were asserting their independence in all aspects of daily life. However, despite this wide globalization, the image of Philip IV (the Fair) of France is often regarded as the epitome of the greed of. However, whether or not he was greedy the King certainly was faced with an economic crisis that was triggered by the country's current debts which was exacerbated by the recent military campaigns. In order to address the issue, Philip debased the French coinage by two-thirds. This unpopular decision resulted in violent riots which the King sought (and was granted) refuge in his Knights Templar compound in Paris. It is safe to say that in the eyes of the general public Philip the Fair was an untrustworthy and profit-driven monarch. The moment Pope Clement V retold the incident of the Templars detentions within his public declarations, it was his intention to announce that the King was not influenced by greed and did not intend to take any Templar property. It appears that the majority of people believed the opposite. However, Philip IV is often associated with a different personality trait. There is evidence to suggest that seeing himself as a religious Catholic Philip was motivated to cleanse his Christian world and consequently entered into a variety of conflict. Philip famously pushed the Jews from France. Also, he confronted Pope Boniface VIII with accusations of sodomy and heresy and ultimately bringing him to the ground. The King's attention to spiritual issues was evidently heightened following the demise of his wife Joan I of Navarre in 1305 two years before being arrested by the Knights Templar. Philip could have justified his actions in his own mind thinking that the corruption of the Pope has led to corrupting the army orders accountable only to the Pope. It's also possible Philip was just trying the same method against a different target by using his religious fervor as an excuse.

The original reason for initiating an investigation into those who were Knights Templar was provided by one Esquieu (or Esquin) de Floyran of Beziers. His identity isn't established, however it is possible that he was an escaped Templar and was subsequently exiled by the Order and harboring a grudge against the Order. The first time he contacted the King James II of Aragon who was skeptical of his claims and the same accusations were considered serious from Philip the Fair. There is evidence to suggest that the King also communicated the details to Pope Clement V, who told him to put off the action to a later date, which Philip did not take (Barber 2006, 64-65). Philip V also knew that he was the only person to take on the case. Guillaume de Nogaret had already established himself as a trustworthy and competent advisor. Born in 1260, and trained in the law field as well as the law, he was instrumental in the fierce battle against the pope Boniface VIII. Just prior to the arrests by the Knights Templar within France, de Nogaret was named Chancellor of the Kingdom . This was as a sign of appreciation for his previous efforts as well as a necessity for an boost in authority to carry out a greater job.

King Philip IV was aware the fact that, as a French monarch, he didn't have the authority to detain and convict members of a military religious organization under the authority of the Pope. Legality in this particular case was created through the use of Guillaume Humbert of Paris, who was a Dominican friar and the head of the Inquisition in France. In documents from the time the man is identified simply by the name of Guillaume from Paris (the last name is deleted as a sign of vows to monastics). The Inquisitor title permitted him to make use of the entire resources and staff that were available to the Inquisition and to also serve as the pope's deputy. In the days of the trials Guillaume also held the highly prestigious post as the royal confessor. There is certain that the he was involved in the same circle as Philip the Fair concerning the scandal that involved the Templars. Guillaume was wisely mentioned in the original order of arrest as "our dear Brother of Christ G. of Paris Inquisitor of heretical immorality with the approval of Pope Francis" (Barber 2002 246).

On the 13th of October 1307, many Knights Templar were arrested in France by the agents from Philip IV. Philip IV. They were accused of denial of Christ as well as throwing a spit on the cross as well as kissing the receptors the navel, the mouth as well as the bottom of the spine in initiation ceremonies and an institutionalized homosexuality and belief in the "bearded male head." The Templars were subjected to torture, which was considered at the time an acceptable method to gather evidence. The testimony of witnesses from outside was not heard and even a thorough investigation of the property of the Order was unable to yield any evidence of incrimination. The defense for The Knights Templar was based solely upon confessions retrieved from the police.

It was not unusual for torture to be used in the trial was not new. These practices have been accepted by the church from 1252 at the very least, in which Pope Innocent IV, in the bull Ad Extirpanda allowed the use of torture only in the pursuit of evidence from those who were heretics. The royal arrest warrants on which the agents of the King were acting in the month of October 1307 clearly indicated that severe treatment was required in this circumstance: "Despite the fact that there are some who may be guilty, and others innocent, due to the seriousness of this situation, in which the truth can't be exposed by any other means and since a fervent suspicion has been poured on everyone and everyone involved, it is only fitting to ensure that any innocent among them, they ought to be examined in a furnace of gold, and cleared through the appropriate process of judicial scrutiny" (Barber 2002 246). The efficacy of torture methods used against the Knights Templar is apparent from the statements that Brother Ponsard de Gisy. He during his testimony on the 27th of November 1309, described his condition in the previous interrogation, in terms of being ready to answer whatever was demanded of him (ibid, 299.). There are a variety of reasons why torture sessions were not recorded however a careful examination of depositions offers a glimpse of what transpired. It has been observed that, for example, in the initial phase of the trial, the only statements that Templars have denied all charges against the Order were recorded on days that its top officials also appeared in court. In the end, chief inquisitors, and possibly torture specialists were not present during certain interrogations (Pernoud, the 116th).

The Knights Templar felt that legal action against them was only able to have been taken without the approval of the Pope, that was evidently not there. The reaction of the newly installed Cardinal Clement V was not entirely uniform or uncompromising. He did express his displeasure regarding the issue in a letter to King Charles V, however the King did not heed his advice by any significant papal decision (excommunication by Philip IV, for instance). The reasons behind this were complicated. Although Clement was furious with the blatant disregard for his authority but he did not have a conviction to protect those who were Knights Templar for their own reasons. Reforms of a serious nature were in the pipeline for orders from the military following the loss of the Holy Land, as they had too much power and resources, but they had no proper way to utilize their power. Thus, the King's attack against his Knights Templar was a bit timely and could even be useful. However there was a serious possibility that the Church could be forced to surrender Templar property and lands for that of the French crown (Partner 72). It is worth noting that rumors circulated for a long time Middle Ages that the Pope's abdication of the Knights Templar resulted from his devotion toward the king Philip IV who had been influential in getting the throne of Pope Francis for his friend two years before the notorious arrests. The pope was repeatedly pressured. Clement V chose to follow a course that made dissolution of the Order unavoidable, while in the process trying to portray himself as a responsible and reasonable pope. This meant a general acceptance of the King's attack on the Templars and taking steps to assist in the investigation, or at the very least slow the pace of the events. In the month of November 1307, Clement V ordered that Knights Templar be detained and investigated throughout Christendom. In the months following it was it was the Holy See also made continuous efforts to play an active involvement in the ongoing investigation. The King's position was somewhat diminished when, on the 27th of December 1307, the Templar Grand Master made the decision to retract his previous declarations (according to some sources, this was a public affair that saw de Molay demonstrated signs of torture on his arms). In response to this decision the Pope suspended the power of the inquisitors. after a long-running battle between the King as well as his representatives the Pope was capable of having the majority of Templars transported to Poitiers which was where he held his court. There has been speculation that these individuals were selected to portray their fellow Knights Templar in the least positive way (Barber 2006 120-121). These were typically lower-ranking members of the Order, and a few might have harbored an animus towards the Order. The top leaders of the Knights Templar who were also traveling to Poitiers were taken into Chinon Castle in an apparent attempt to disqualify papal inquires.

Between June 28 and July 1st 1308, a specially designated commission heard confessions from the 72 Templars who were brought to Poitiers. The confessions of the Templars included apologies for throwing a spit on the cross, and denial of Christ at the time of their initiation and the same confessions which were taken during previous examinations conducted by the inquisitors. According to Clement V, these were serious and infuriating things, yet they were not heresies. On July 2, a public consortial was held in which the Pope delivered the "plenary absolution for the Templars who admitted their sins and had asked forgiveness from the church" (Frale 2004 125.). In August of that same year, the Pope took his deputy for Chinon where the chiefs of the Knights Templar, including their Grand Master, were detained. The knights of high rank were also being interrogated by Papal Envoys cardinals Berenger Fredol, Etienne de Suisy and Landolfo Bracacci. Knights' confessions together with absolution announcements in formal form were recorded in the document called Chinon Parchment. Chinon

Chinchment (or Chinon Chart). It could be thought that this was the perfect moment to put an end to the trial of Knights Templar in its tracks. Of course, this was not the case. Clement V proved that he had the freedom to exercise his authority in matters of spirituality however he was not able (or not willing) to take the legal issue against the Templars from the grasp of King Philip's advisors, and to bring all prisoners into control of the Church. In the end, many Templars who resolved their spiritual issues in thirteen08's summer ultimately died in the hands of the King.

The Pope positioned him as "good shepherd" The Pope issued an official decree titled Faciens misericordiam ("Granting forgiveness"). The name Clement was selected for the name by Raymond Bertrand de Got while being elevated to the throne of Pope Benedict in 1305 aptly sounded to convey forgiveness and kindness. In the bull that was issued, the Pope spoke of the things that transpired over the last year, stating that both rank-and file Templars as well as the eminent

Members of the Order were granted pardon for their sins. In the same breath, Clement recognized the need for further investigation and requested a Church meeting to be held in to decide the fate for the Knights Templar. He also removed the inquisition's authority in the matter.

It was most likely this odd circumstance of being investigated and being forgiven, that caused the last flurry of rebellion from the Templars. The legal basis for this attempt to clean the name of the Order was provided through Pierre de Bologna (1270-1310?). In contrast to the majority of Templars, de Bologna was highly educated. It could be that he been educated in the field of law at Bologna, Italy. De Bologna argued that torture was not able to provide reliable evidence. The defense was confronted with a ferocious punishment: the knights who had retracted their testimony were burned at the stake as the relapsed heretics on May 12 1310. Philip IV supposedly made an attempt to appear during this execution.

The council in Vienne in 1312 the decision on the fate of Knights Templar was resolved.

It was decided to disband the Order on the pretense that its reputation was severely damaged, despite absence of any formal condemnation by the Church and Pope. It was decided that the Knights Templar possessions were to be handed over to Hospitallers and, from that point on, no one could claim to be as a Templar or wear the uniform of the Order, to avoid excommunication. The decisions were brutal and abrupt, as Clement V had to quiet the voices of those not in support of his decision.

The Order was officially inactive The fate of its ex-members had to be determined. For the majority of Templars it meant either enduring long prison sentences or transferred to a remote monastery belonging to another monastic order. In the spring of 1314, the sentencing committee decided to decide on the leaders of the Knights Templar, Hugues de Pairaud and Geoffroi de Gonneville accepted their sentence of life imprisonment in the King's prison , without speaking one word. Jacques de Molay, the Grand Master of the Order along with Geoffroi de Charney instantly denied the previous confessions and evidence (on the official grounds for which they had already been granted pardon by Chinon!) They claimed they were innocent and they were members of the Order of the Knights Templar was "pure and holy" (Barber 2006, 3).The King's decision was quick. Both were brought by the police to Ile des Javiaux in the Seine and were burned to death as relapsed heretics, on March 18th 1314. According to legend, Jacques de Molay proclaimed that within a short time, the King and Pope will be subject to God's judgement and face the consequences of their actions. This story could have been told just a few days following the execution of two Templar martyrs due to the fact that Clement V only outlived them by one month, and Philip the Fair died in November of that year, presumably due to an incident in the hunt. It was the year that Inquisitor Guillaume from Paris, was also killed that year.

The demise of Knights Templar order in France was brutal and brutal. And in other nations, the Templars received more exclusive treatment. In general, only in those areas where torture was used in interrogations was a fact, are there confessions incriminating to the person being accused. In England the use of torture was not utilized in the case of Templars until 1311 and, even at that time, two of the most prominent Members of the Order William of la More and Imbert Blanke continued to not admit to their guilt (Barber 2006 228). Then in the Iberian peninsula, the Order was basically transformed under the name the Order of Christ.

The Knights Templar were simply too massive to go away without having an impact. This resulted in a variety of theories suggesting that the Order survived events of the 14th century, and then continued in a way that was not apparent to historical studies. Today , there are a variety of organisations that claim to have a descendant to that of Knights Templar, but adequate evidence appears to be missing in every instance. The most intriguing document that is frequently cited as source of proof of lineage going back to that of the Knights Templar to the Masonic movement in the 1800s was the known as the Larmenius Charter. It is believed to have been composed by John Mark Larmenius who supposedly had a close relationship with Jacques de Molay as the Grand Master of the Knights Templar. The document was written in the form of a Latin which is much more refined as well as "classical" in character as opposed to the more common medieval documents. There are some noteworthy historical anachronisms that attract attention. For example the Larmenius Charter contains the phrase Ad majorem Dei Gloriam ("To the splendor that of God") that is believed to have been used only once by Pope Gregory the Great in the 6th century. It was also prior to when Ignatius Loyola formulated the Jesuits famous motto. Yet, the writer of the Charter makes use of these phrases in a way that makes them appear standard and formulaic. Another notable phrase is privilegia conti ("I conferred privilegia contortii"). The formula is only found (typically in plural form - contulimus) in diplomas issued by universities of the later period. It is possible that the person who wrote the Larmenius Charter had such a diploma. Furthermore, Larmenius calls himself hyerosolimitanus and says "of Jerusalem." One is left to be wondering when was the last time Knights Templar were allowed to be in Jerusalem! In addition, the document's ambiguous authenticity makes it much more likely seen as a forgery.

Although there is no evidence-based proof of the Templar connection but the legacy of the legendary military order lives in a variety of modern organisations that display a spirit of fraternity and dedication to their causes. The modern Masonic as well as non-Masonic Templars have a keen interest in the history of the medieval Knights Templar and are constantly urging academic researchers to pay attention to the Order's history. This is often overlooked because of the stigma associated with Romanticist mythology that is associated with the Order.

Chapter 10: The Chinon Parchment

The missing piece

It is long believed from many scholars that, when the Pope Clement V was finally able to conduct an interrogation of a large section of Knights Templar at Poitiers, in his summer in 1308, he also was able get access to some of the order's leadership. Jacques de Molay, Grand Master of the Order; Raymbaud de Caron, preceptor of Outremer; Hugues de Pairaud preceptor from France; Geoffroi de Gonneville preceptor for Aquitaine and Poitou as well as Geoffroi de Charney Preceptor of Normandy and Poitou, were held in Chinon's fortress. Chinon which was just 60 miles from Poitiers. The bull Faciens Misericordiam, promulgated in August of 1308 The Pope stated that due to the being in poor health, some of the prisoners with high-profile status, the journey to them was difficult so three trusted cardinals were sent to listen to the testimony of the knights and, if needed they would offer them papal absolution for their transgressions. The cardinals found the leaders to be guilty of the same offenses similar to the Templars who were interrogated in Poitiers earlier in the summer. After begging forgiveness on their knees with hands folded in prayer The leadership in the Knights Templar Order were granted absolution "because the Church is not able to keep her bosom open to anyone returning," as Clement V stated. The bull also stated that documents pertaining to this significant event were confirmed by public notaries.

Along with the records of the hearings at Poitiers this data provided an almost complete picture of the Pope's intention to forgive all individuals Templars for their likely non-Catholic actions. But the actual document that could be the result of the hearings at Chinon could not be located, leading some experts to think that the Pope just lied about the subject. in 2001 Barbara Frale, a researcher at the Vatican Secret Archives, located an unfiled parchment with reports of provincial inquiries commanded through Clement V in 1308. The document included the names of the three cardinals who were summoned for Chinon in 1308 by the Pope to question members of the Templar chiefs: Berenger (Fredol), Etienne (de Suisy) as well as Landolfo (Brancacci). After examination, the document proved to be original document on parchment with the seals of the cardinals. It also outlined the events that transpired at Chinon in the month of August 1308. The proof of papal absolution given to the Knights Templar was now complete. These findings were first reported in 2003 by Barbara Frale in 2003. In 2007, to commemorate the Templars arrests and trial, the Vatican created a high-end replica of various documents relating to the trial and included the Chinon Parchment. The only copies that were numbered of the limited edition called Processus contra Templarios were published (one unnumbered copy was reserved for the Pope) and the exceptional quality of the workmanship used in each copy was evident in the price of nearly 6000 euros. This decision by the Holy See is being widely taken up, but it's appropriate to say that it did not help improve accessibility of these precious papers to the public at large. While the documents in this collection generally endorse an idea that the Pope took action out of concern about the Templars their spiritual standing however, they also contain numerous disturbing details and facts. The question of whether or not these events were the result of torture or intimidation techniques is a different matter completely, but concerns of propriety could have been a factor in the Vatican's decision to restrict the information on the trials - in making it a little more accessible by placing Processus against Templarios into the hands of non-interested book collectors the subject, or in the best instances, by having the edition given to the rare book depositories of large libraries. It's not a doubt that a cheaper edition is a popular choice for experts and fans as well as offering the chance to correct typographical mistakes that unfortunately aren't in this incredibly expensive two-volume set.

The winter of 2006,, when the interest of the public in Chinon Parchment was at its highest, and the public interest in Chinon

Chinchment reached its peak I decided to create myself a translation in order to meet the needs of a variety of scholars and Templar enthusiasts from all over the world. This translation was not designed to serve as the sole source to the document, because I had hoped that a more polished translation would be forthcoming from an expert with expertise in Medieval history. Instead, my rough online translation quickly became the standard source for students of the time. After the text was published in its entirety as an appendix in a book concerning The Vatican's Secrets I decided that it was ideal to write my own version in order to ensure that my translation was clear, fluid and as precise as is possible. It took a long time for this concept to be realized. It's not perfect However, nothing is perfect. To assist researchers who would like to read an original version of Chinon Parchment it has also been included within this volume. The Latin text has been reproduced with Barbara Frale's permission. It is included in this book in the original form, transcribed as published by the author in Il papato e il proceso in the

Templari. Templari. L'inedita assoluzione di Chinon alla luce della Diplomatica pontificia, Roma: Viella, 2003. Certain editorial modifications were created based on the text that was published in Processus against Templarios. At several times, I looked up the facsimile copy Chinon Parchment provided with the publication.

A brief overview of the document

Chinon Parchment Chinon Parchment is an enormous Vellum piece that measures 700x580 mm. It is in generally good condition, but there is small damage, perhaps from the flames that are visible in the upper portion of the paper. Three seals are attached to the parchment as a means of verification. The document was created by utilizing notes from examinations. The Register Avignonese 48 from the Vatican Secret Archives contains those actual notes, which were released in Processus against Templarios.

Introduction. Following the cardinals with responsibility for the investigation identify their titles and names, the document is opened with a lengthy introduction explaining the purpose and nature of the document. The document is meant to be a record for the public of an inquiry commissioned through Pope Clement V with the aim to discover the truth about the accusations that were made against those who were the Knights Templar by the King of France. The cardinals make evident that the proceedings at Chinon were intended to be an essential second phase of investigations already taking to Poitiers. The necessary steps to be taken to ensure the authenticity for the certificate (due diligence as well as the presence of witnesses and notaries as well as the subsequent attachment to individual seals) are as well announced.

The examination of Raymbaud deCaron on the 17th of August 1308. The person who is questioned swears an oath after placing his hands upon the gospel. It is observed that his hands physically placed his hand on the book - an important point of distinction. The test is based on an outline, which is likely known to all contestants. The first question pertaining to the date and time of the initiation ceremony in the Order of the Knights Templar will allow for a brief account which is likely intended for the purpose of helping "loosen the shoulders" the person who is taking part. De Caron admits to being required to confess to Christ right after the ceremony of initiation, but states that he then admitted to the was a sin. De Caron denies any personal involvement in homosexual behavior and denies the tendency of the Order to commit the sin. De Caron is unsure whether the majority of Templars were admitted to the Order by the same ceremony, as he has only seen the initiation of two or three people. He maintains that he had no prior knowledge of spitting on a cross, worshipping heads that resemble idols or kisses of any kind aside from one kiss to the mouth that he received at the time of his ceremony of initiation. Following making the confessional, a formal statement is given, according to the formula, which Raymbaud de Caron validated his declaration and verified its authenticity and credibility. Then, he requests forgiveness for his sins. The attention is then drawn to the visible signs of repentance (standing on one's knees and with fingers folded) and swearing to the Gospel again. The cardinals' discussions to de Caron are concluded as they officially absolve the man of his sins by lifting the excommunication sentence which was automatically imposed upon him after he had committed the wrongs.

Examen of Geoffroi de Charney on the 17th of August 1308. The person who is examined swears an oath. The story of his initiation of the Order of the Knights Templar includes condemning Christ (he explicitly states that this was not something was done with heartfelt conviction, but through only words) while kissing the receiver both on his chest and mouth by wearing a dress, as a sign to show respect. De Charney isn't sure whether the other brothers also went through the same process. He himself was the initiator of one brother by following the same procedure, however, he also initiated many novices without the incriminating addition. De Charney also claims that he sought absolution by the patriarchal Patriarch of Jerusalem. De Charney says he has no information regarding the practice of spilling blood on the cross, or the act of kissing or the vice of sodomy, and the worship of a head-like idol. Maybe spotting some contradictions between the responses (at at least two types of kisses, for example were previously discussed by the person who is defending) Investigators inquire the deponent if they believe that other brothers were also initiated to the order by the same procedure. Deponent believes this was actually the case but nothing can be certain, as a result of the secrecy associated with the ceremonies. The test is accompanied by the exact formulas which verify the authenticity of the testimony. credibility, relating the witness's desire to forgive and grant the deponent's absolution. In comparison to the testimony of de Caron's test the part that follows is abbreviated.

Examen of Geoffroi de Gonneville on the 17th of August 1308. The candidate swears an oath. The story of his initiation tells that following the ceremony, the deponent was asked to be adamant about Christ in the manner depicted on the crucifix that is depicted in the book. If he did not denounce Christ and was then offered an alternative: he did not have to issue the denunciation, but in case others brothers inquired about the matter, he was to inform them that he actually had a smear against Christ at the time of his ceremony of initiation. The deponent was then requested to spit at the crucifix. He was unable to do. If he was asked to throw a spit at the hands of the person who was receiving the request when it was covered by the crucifix not to (for the fear that the hand could be taken away) and then spat in the vicinity. The defendant is ignorant of the crime of sodomy, the idol-like head, rituals of kissing, and other sexy acts that are reflected in the accusations against Knights Templar. The test is followed by formulas in abbreviated form that prove the credibility and completeness of the testimony and also substantiate the defendant's need to be forgiven and grant the deponent's absolution.

Examen of Hugues de Pairaud, on the 19th of August 1308. The testimonies of the deponent are taken. He recounts that shortly after his induction into the order, he was taken away and was asked to declare his opposition to Christ and was given the Crucifix. After being threatened numerous times, de Pairaud finally did the right thing. But, he was not willing to throw a spit at the cross. He also claims that during the ceremony, he was required be required to kiss the shrine in the lips. He has denied ever being involved in homosexual activities. De Pairaud says that he was the person responsible for initiating more people to join the Order than anyone else. He confesses to having instructed his followers to disown the crucifix, and to kiss him on the bottom of their spines, around the navel, and finally on the lips. He states that he instructed them that if in a position to resist their desire and lust, they should be joined with the brothers in the order. As per de Pairaud, he did not feel a deep conviction in causing the initiates to declare their hatred of Christ. When asked why he chose to do this however, he states that it was the law of the Order, however he would like to see these rules will be repealed. Apart from that, de Pairaud confirms that he actually saw the head, believed to be worshiped by the Templars in Montpelier located in its possession by Brother Pierre Alemandin. He also wishes to abide by his confessions made in Paris in front of an Inspector Guillaume who is from Paris and his substitute. The test will be followed with the exact formulas, which are abbreviated to ensure the credibility and completeness of the confession and also substantiate the person's need to forgive and award the deponent's absolution.

Examen of Jacques de Molay on August 20 1308. The testimonies of the deponent are taken on vow. He acknowledges that when he was formally initiated to the Order of the Knights Templar the order was to be adamant about Christ by spitting on His cross. He states that he had spoken to Him in a way that denounced Him however, only in front of others and did not throw a spit at the cross, however, he did spit near it. De Molay claims that he does not have any information about sodomy's sin as well as the head that resembles an idol and the practice of kissing illicitly within the Order. The short investigation is then followed by abbreviated formulas to verify the authenticity of the testimony, as well as its authenticity, as well as the need for forgiveness, and award the deponent's absolution.

Geoffroi de Gonneville confirms his testimony. On the 20th of August 1308, Geoffroi de gonneville is read his recorded declaration in the native dialect. He affirms his desire to adhere to the testimony he gave in Paris along with his testimony in Paris.

Hugues de Pairaud confirms his testimony. On the 20th of August 1308 Hugues de Pairaud was read his recorded deposition in his native language. He affirms his desire to follow the deposition.

The cardinals' verdict. The three cardinals have ordered the public record of the testimony and deeds mentioned above is prepared through Robert de Condet.

Witnesses present at the examinations are recorded.

Public notaries are required to sign the document. Robert de Condet states that the document was his own in which he outlines the acts and words have been observed by him. He also used his notarial seal. Three other notaries in public confirm that they complied with the actions and testimonies that were described earlier. They also confirm that they have applied their notarial marks on the document.

The issue of Templars" guilt

The Chinon Parchment and earlier testimonies

The Chinon Parchment may be examined from various angles. It is possible to look at its paleographic traits as well as compare its design with similar documents from the same period, or use it to highlight the peculiarities that are characteristic of Medieval Latin, but it is most likely legally based. Its goal was to create an account of important legal proceedings, which demonstrates the guilt of participants and describing how they were determined about their fates by the ruling authorities. In it is clear that from the Chinon Parchment it follows without doubt that the members of the Knights Templar, examined in the month of August 1308 at the hands of pope's envoys admitted their guilt and were granted pardons for their crimes. Thus, the issue of guilt in the real sense is something that is of interest to the majority of Templar researchers greater than, say the nature of writing hands on the document.

Examining knights Templar from papal official during Poitiers and Chinon appear to be fairness. The Templars were investigated by the same authorities who they were obligated to. They were not subjected to threat of torture or intimidation. The apostates who were suspected repeatedly repeated the same confessions received from them prior to. What can this evidence be assessed? What evidence can be found to prove that the Knights actually commit the actions they confessed to? Did their initiation ceremonies be then followed by bizarre denials about Christ and spitting on the cross, and kissing the preceptors in a way that was inappropriate? If so do you have any reason to think that some of the more serious accusations like idols and worship of devils, were founded in fact?

It would be a pity and an act of great indignation to anyone who has been falsely accused of something to not think about the chance that Knights Templar were completely innocent in spite of their testimony given in 1308. It could be a case of an irrational belief of someone who isn't completely objective. However, it is important to keep in mind that when the Templars were interrogated by papal commissioners, they were technically still in the custody of the King's guards. The factor of intimidation was at work. Additionally, there was no motivation to change previous confessions in the present, when just repeating them would guarantee absolution. In 1310, a huge group of Templars resolved to deny their earlier testimony, they were burned to death as rebels who had relapsed. It's an occurrence when inadmissible evidence plays a significant role. only those who keep their innocence and provide more valuable evidence are likely to survive. When a prisoner retracts his confession and denies guilt, they go is no longer an asset but becoming a risk. There is no question of the possibility that Jacques de Molay and Geoffroi de Charney were acutely aware of the tragic turn of fate that fell on their fellow comrades in 1310 after they had retracted their earlier confessions in order to avoid certain death in the month of March 1314. It is also likely that Grandmaster, along with numerous other Templars had a good understanding of medieval law to anticipate the worst if they had behaved differently during the trials in Poitiers or Chinon during the heat of summer 1308. Refusing to admit guilt could have been dangerous and foolish at a time that there was still a small chance to save the Order. It is possible to conclusively say that neither the rank-and-file Knights Templar nor the Order's leaders were in a favorable situation to protect themselves.

The arrested Templars were not able to be honest (if they differed from their earlier forced confessions) However, there are some divergences between the accounts given at Paris in the autumn of 1307 and the ones given during the summer of 1308 in Poitiers as well as Chinon. For instance the time Geoffroi de Charney recounted the tale of his induction into the Order, he claimed that to show respect, he kissed his receiving brother's chest and around the mouth by wearing garments. But, when he recounted the same story to the inquisitors a few months earlier De Charney stated that he did not kiss the navel's receptor (Michelet II . 295). Geoffroi de Gonneville in his testimony at Chinon suggests that he resisted spitting on the cross even after being instructed not to, despite the fact that the hands of the receptor were covering the cross. Believing that the receptor would immediately take his hand away, causing the initiator to spit on the cross, de Gonneville reportedly spat out of the cross which was covered. The earlier and longer testimony does not indicate that the receptor caused him to spill his blood on his hands as they covered his cross (Michelet II 399, refer to Appendix 2.). Brother Raymbaud de Caron, in his initial testimony, included an extremely important detail that did not appear in his confession in Chinon. Prior to the time of the initiation the Templars presented him with a crucifix and told him: "If you want to be accepted in the order of Templars, then you have to disbelieve him" (Michelet II 374 (see Appendix 2.). The initiation was said to have taken place during the presence of the de Caron's cousin Archbishop de Carpentras. The confession of de Caron at Chinon however, on the other hand, reveals an account of the young Raymbaud telling what he'd committed to the archbishop, after the ceremony had concluded.

It is clear that the detained Templars weren't in any mental or physical state that would allow them to repeat their confessions in full. This is especially true when the confessions were not referring to anything from their own thoughts, rather they were made by intimidation and pressure. Also, it evident that the papal commission in Chinon did not seem to be as interested in finding the whole truth as they could be (assuming that of course that they believed in the Templars even at all). Even if the cardinals do not have records of prior interrogations (which I am sure they did) they might have observed the internal contradictory confessions. For example, Geoffroi de Charney, who in his Chinon confession admitted that he had kissed the chest receptor as well as on the lips and then later claimed that he was unaware of any kisses.

The papal legates did not seem to be interested in investigating certain leads the imprisoned Templars were offering. For example, when they inquired of Hugues de Pairaud if he was aware of "the "idol-like head" the man in question immediately responded that he knew, and that he actually witnessed it in Montpeliers with the Brother Pierre Alemandin. The inquisitors of Paris were keen enough to question de Pairaud about the appearance of this supposed idol . They were told it was a four-legged creature Two legs in the front, two on the face side and two in the back (a somewhat odd method of describing an idol, but without even trying to describe the facial characteristics or hair, however one should be aware that all Templars who shared any information concerning the idol gave very different and bizarre descriptions). It is fascinating that of the five Templars who were interrogated in Chinon by papal representatives, Hugues de Pairaud was only the one to make reference to his previous deposition, specifically referring to his deposition that everything he had said to the inquisitors or inquisitor during his time in Paris was authentic. If we take a look at the deposition de Pairaud gave in his first interview, we find something atypical. When he was asked if everyone in the order was treated in the way he described (i.e. with refusals to believe in Christ or kissing receptors placed on the mouth, within the navel as well as at the spine's base), de Pairaud replied that he didn't think that way. The interrogation was then stopped, and following a break, de Pairaud declared that he was unable to comprehend the question correctly and reacted in a wrong way. He later stated that the Members of the Order had been greeted in the same manner as that was described (Barber 2006, 257). It is believed that the interruption in the interrogation was a method of the purpose of torturing the person being interrogated. De Pairaud's comment on being a four-legged Templar head is also made following this interruption. The interrogation at Paris is likely to have left quite an impression de Pairaud if he so strongly pleaded with the commission at Chinon to keep the matter under consideration. However, even if the cardinals were able to access a copy of his initial testimony however, their lack of interest appears odd. There is probably more to discover concerning what happened to the Templar head, as long as de Pairaud was telling the truth and was not talking about an incident he had been forced speak under pressure.

If cardinals truly would like to find some reason for the unconventional ceremony of initiation, they might have taken a lesson about Geoffroi of Gonneville. In the course of the proceedings in Paris the French Cardinal said that according to the rumours that a particular Grand Master, who was held by the Saracens were ordered to incorporate a suggestion of similar treatment into the ceremony of initiation for the Order in exchange for the requirement for his release from jail. The other possibility is his belief that the his brother Roncelin (presumably, Roncelin de Fos) might have brought corruption into the life of the Order and it could be grand master Thomas Berard who was responsible for the creation of those incriminating practices. De Gonneville also suggested that the denials of Christ might have been made as a remembrance or imitation of St. Peter who denied three times Jesus Christ as his Savior (hoc fit ad instar seu in remembering beati petri qui abnegavit Christum ter) (Michelet II.400.). The papal commission in Chinon was completely unprepared to request that de Gonneville elaborate on this fascinating subject.

In the end when The Grand Master, Jacques de Molay himself was present before the commission His deposition, which was governed by cardinals' inquiries proved to be the most concise of all. Contrary to the inquisitors from Paris and Rome, the papal envoys did not bother to inquire whether, for example when he was the first to initiate new Knights to the Order (which in the deposition dated the 24th of October, 1307 did he ask someone else to set the novices off "to perform the task that was required") (Barber 2005 252).

One could get an impression that the commission performed its duties in a sloppy manner. The testimonies were taken into consideration, and if they contained incriminating evidence (which was likely provided that the prisoner were able to repeat their confessions with some congruity) The members in the Order had accused of venial sins and acquitted upon the spot. In light of this process it is fascinating that according to de Gonneville's testimony before of cardinals, his crimes could include only a deceive himself about the defamation of Christ (whom he didn't condemn!) and spilling on the cross. And if papal envoys took the time to study de Gonneville's initial statement, they'd find something completely bizarre and bizarre: when the person who is the receiver gives de Gonneville promise that he will inform all others who asked him whether he actually committed a denial of Christ in the initiation ceremony when the novice is required to take an oath in his belief in the Holy Gospel - hardly a behaviour that one would expect from an infidel. It's not too far-fetched to conclude that, solely based on his confessions to Chinon Geoffroi de Gonneville was not guilty but only through an association.

The Chinon parchment is therefore evidence of an investigation where the participants were hesitant to defend themselves, while the examiners were not interested in their testimony. There are two aspects, however, which allow one to admit the Templars in their innocence in light of this document, particularly in how they framed their prior confessions. First, any contradictions or discrepancies in testimony are more likely to be a sign that witnesses are lying, in this case, lying about their guilt. The second reason is that the investigators' inability to show curiosity in depositions indicates an implicit understanding that these testimony is not admissible because they are not admitting guilt. It could be an implicit agreement between the two sides, since this arrangement would have been acceptable for both parties. The Templars were prepared to repeat their earlier testimony however they could because the main difference was the fact that these testimonies were required to follow by papal absolution, possibly an initial step towards an acquittal. The cardinals, on contrary could assert the authority of the Pope, without causing offence to Philip the Fair by dismantling an legal case that he was "banking" upon.

Chapter 11: The Interpretation Of The Evidence

Given what has been discussed, the total innocent of Knights Templar seems to be an enviable theory. Yet the amount of proof against them despite being taken under duress is overwhelming. There are many pages worth of statements provided by the members where they confess to numerous violations. It's difficult to shake off the notion that "there was something going on."

In the depositions that are still in existence, there is an interesting comment that was made by a sergeant-brother whose name is Jean (Johannes) and whose surname is transcribed variously to be Senandi, Senanti or Cenaudi (Mich. II, pp. 136-141). He was a preceptor in the home of Knights Templar in la Fouillouse His initiation report included a remark about condemning Christ and spitting on the cross and being told to be gay with fellow members from the order. Brother Jean was also reported to have been present at the initiation ceremonies for various other Templars and witnessed similar processes, and also told the inquisitors that these actions were unpalatable to him (sibi displicebant predicta). Then, he made a declaration that stated that Jacques de Molay, before being appointed Grand Master, addressed an assembly regarding his plan to "root out" some things were deemed to be offensive (aliqua qu'erentia in order sibi displicencia) and, if they didn't, they could eventually be detrimental to members of the Knights Templar. However, it is unlikely (if we accept this claim even a little) the fact that de Molay would have spelled out his concerns related to this issue during an ordinary meeting. Brother Jean himself admitted to the inquirers that when he attempted to find answers on the subject the advice was to remain "deaf blind, mute, and deaf," because as a sergeant, he was disregarded by the knights in any case. Should de Molay himself came close to being a whistleblower in the presence of sergeants and knights equally, Templar testimonies would have be swarming with evidence. It's not the certainty the fact that de Molay spoke of anything which had to do with morals or initiation practices that were illegal but at the end the deposition Senandi stated that he had was able to hear his Grand Master as well as other witnesses speak of the same illegal methods he had admitted to having witnessed. It could be that he felt under pressure to provide this clarification. The article that linked brother Jean's memories of de Molay's words with the present scenario could be a fulfillment of the prophecy of harm that was caused by the order. Whatever the reason for Jacques de Molay's worry was at the time that the Templars were in very deep trouble.

De Molay's claimed condemnation of morally wrong practices Let us concentrate on Templar testimonials themselves. Particularly, the promotion of homosexuality inside the Order is something numerous Templars confessed to being an aspect of their (and other people's) induction ceremony. This deviation from what might have been considered to be an appropriate ritual is different from spilling blood on the cross and denial of Christ. The initiates were not required to regularly spit on the cross or to denounce Christ for a long time as proof of their participation to the Order. The newly formed Templars could simply admit to their actions and seek forgiveness. The priests of the Order would ensure that they had not committed any serious sins, and they were to spend the rest their lives wondering what this whole mess was about (Frale, 165,). Being told that homosexual relationships are acceptable (as as one cannot keep oneself chaste) is not a crime in itself and didn't require confession. But if these guidelines were adhered to with any degree of discipline, homosexuality could be the norm within the Knights Templar. However, it appears that the Templars strictly adhered to authority didn't apply to this particular situation! Jean Senandi stated in spite of being informed sexual relations could be had with other Templars but he never did whatsoever and had never had any information about anyone involved in sodomy, besides an unidentified presbyter, who was deceased, who was said to have "misused" males from the secular world. Overall, of the roughly

11,000 surviving testimony from the trials, only six testify to homosexual relationships (Frale, 164,). In light of the fact that among the many soldiers who joined the military ranks, some were homosexuals and bisexual. This is evidence that no matter the information that new recruits were informed following the formal initiation ceremony, it had no impact on their conduct and actions when they joined the Knights Templar. If this is the case with regard to sexual relations between couples, which were practically a requirement for some the new recruits, it's also the case for bizarre manipulations with the cross and refusals to believe in Christ that Templar new members were required to undergo as per their own testimonies.

It is important to note that the Pope did not appear to seriously consider any allegations apart from those related with the induction ceremony that, if taken as a whole considered to be legitimate was not a case of heresy. In announcing his dissolution from the Knights Templar in the bull Vox in Excelso, Clement V was only able to speak with confidence regarding the offenses that occurred during the initiation ceremony. He quoted lengthy passages of the Bible and referred to more serious crimes, like idolatry, but not giving any evidence concrete of the Templars guilty. The Pope also declared that a substantial part of his cardinals believed it was appropriate that "the Order should be given the opportunity to defend itself and it was not able to be condemned in light of the evidence presented thus far, regarding the heresies which were the subject of the investigation" (Barber 2002, 313.). This meant that Clement V was forced to acknowledge that "legal procedure against the Order has to date is not able to allow its canonical denial for heresy by a clear phrase" (ibid.). The reason given for dissolution of the Knights Templar was the presumed impossibleness of ever clearing the name of the Order, which was smacked with so many allegations.

In the present, the only allegations against the Knights Templar that appeared credible to skeptical (albeit not totally impartial) modern minds were centered around the Order's initiation procedures. In the event that Pope Francis believed these specific accusations made against the Templars and the essence of their crime would have seemed to him as a bizarre type of apostasy which was not a factor in the Knights Templar daily activities. In normal circumstances, these crimes could have been addressed by penances and absolutions. However, the truthfulness of these allegations could be in doubt (as it was reportedly questioned by cardinals during the Council of Vienne, many of whom knew how King Philip had used similar accusations on Pope Boniface VIII). The general confusion, the severe treatment, torture intimidation, and even a false belief of forgiveness may have influenced the knights who were imprisoned to follow exactly the same pattern as suggested from the trial. Furthermore, the current Templar testimony regarding their supposed practices of initiation "contain an insufficient explanation as to the reasons they performed these actions, and they show no willingness to defend their actions"

(Barber Process 303). Does anyone have a rational approach to look at this bizarre set of evidence, other than to dismiss it completely?

It could be that the setting in which the Templars' alleged illicit activities could provide clues about their significance. Incorporating new members into military groups of any kind is always associated with customs that range from harmless mockery to violence and violence. But what we find in Templars their testimonies is distinct from mere hazing since actions that appear to degrade and shame new members were confined to the exact moment of their induction being in essence a part of the formal initiation ceremony. The ceremonies of initiation often include components whose purpose is unclear and their meaning is largely unclear to some of the participants. There is a theory that initially Templar rookies faced the type of treatment they would have faced when they were captured by Muslims They would have been ordered to reject Christ and even spit on the cross. According to Barbara Frale, Templar followers were interested in the reactions of new recruits to such an eerie conclusion of their initiation ceremonies "The test exposed the man's character which was this moment that pride, courage determination, determination and the ability to control oneself emerged as essential traits to be an Templar who was destined for combat and a career in command" (Frale, 1767). With time but the reason of this tradition was obscured, and more strange and disturbing aspects were added. At first glance, it seems amazing to think that Knights Templar could have forgotten the reason, the intent, and the right method of conducting an after-initiation test which was at one point developed and may have proved beneficial at some point in time. But, considering the usual confidentiality that the Templars had to preserve in specific regions (often justified) it's not surprising that this alleged test for initiation was kept secret throughout the entire time. Actually, the effectiveness of this test was contingent on the recruits' inadequacy of the existence of this test. This is why brother Jean Sanandi was deemed that he was deaf blind, and blind! It is true that even a Templar candidate with only a little notion of the bizarre consequences of his forthcoming initiation would not have been prepared to be ready for it like it were a test that was specific to him. This particular piece of information might have been among the most secretive secrets within the Knights Templar. As time passed, and the Order was more proficient in recruitment of prospective members, this test may have been abandoned but the process was not stopped. The Templars secret might be deemed useless and redundant. The breaking point in the tradition chain could also have been triggered by catastrophic defeats suffered by the Knights Templar on many occasions which included the devastating losses of soldiers during the battles of La Forbie and Mansurah. In the end, when the time came it was impossible to find anyone alive who could have disclosed the reason for the Templars their post-initiation rituals to the investigation team. In fact, only a handful of Templar depositions try to provide the context to the supposed rituals that led to accusations against the Order. They sound like thoughts or vague memories which suggests that the whole affair was an investigation, an act of satire or the result of additions that the order's laws by a fraudulent Grand Master.

The charges that dealt with irregularities in the initiation ceremony were typically acknowledged in the Knights Templar during their trials however, other admissions were not able to demonstrate consistency. It's therefore not surprising to find that prosecutor decided to add new charges into the case to ensure that the alleged irregularities in the ceremony could be viewed as "gateway" violations. Unforgettable crimes was bound to follow refusals to believe in Christ spilling blood at the altar of Christ, as well as indecent kisses! Rumors and reports included Satan worship, systematic killings of children born illegitimately from The Knights Templar as well as the most sinister types of folk magic, for example, eating the cremated ashes of dead comrades to show their strength and courage. In all the accusations which were not connected to the initiation ceremony , only the worship of a specific "head" was often acknowledged. The accounts of the head were varied, and it is very possible that the accounts illustrate the fact that the Knights Templar were in possession of various saintly relics (Nicholson 146-449). Another theory, recently endorsed by Barbara Frale, suggests that the Order held in its possession the object that is now known in the form of the Shroud of Turin. In the liturgies that it was displayed at only the top half of the shroud's image was clearly visible. Because the nature of the relic's contents was secret or not known to the Templars and their followers, it gave way to many speculative theories.

These theories, while bordering on speculation, offer an reasons for the most persistent topics in the Templars testimony. As with any legal case the presence of motivation or opportunity doesn't automatically mean guilt. It is widely recognized that prosecution wasn't capable of presenting even one single piece of evidence that could prove the most innocent claims about those who were

Knights Templar: no idol-like heads, and no secret laws that governed the order were found.

Retractions of 1314

It is a logical reality the fact Jacques de Molay was dishonest or at Chinon 1308 where he confessed to non-conformist practices of the Knights Templar, or in 1314, when de Molay declared his order was clean and innocent before being burned to death. It is not more logical to believe that the Master was granted papal absolution as a reward for dishonesty, and was willing to sacrifice his life in order to be honest? One could argue the possibility that de Molay and de Charney knew that the Order to be corrupt, but desired to give it an honorable reputation. If that were the case what would have happened if they had decided to be killed in the stake for affirming the innocence of an organization that was already been disbanded, abiding by the consequences of their deceitful lies? Would they have been concerned about the reputation by their fellow Knights Templar in the future? Maybe it was, but only in the event that they really were determined to make their views acknowledged. There was nothing more cause that demanded the sacrifice of a person, and it isn't easy to create an accurate psychological profile that could be suitable for two people who choose to commit suicide with violence because they believed the information to be untrue.

It is often suggested it is possible that regardless of Templars their guilt or lack of guilt de Molay and de Charney just wanted to end their miserable life in prison. In this case they likely were not required to wait for the two years following the Order's dissolution to announce its innocence. it should have been evident that to these two Templar martyrs that their punishment would be anything other than an extended prison sentence.

Self-sacrifice could have been an option de Molay and de Charney thought that the Order had been dissolved and the Order, which was stripped of its authority and possessions, was forced to hide? In the event of such a scenario they could still have a chance of being released as respected members of the Knights Templar Order. However choosing to die to spread the message of the Order's innocence been of no consequence to those brothers that survived, as they would have experienced the truth firsthand. A martyrdom to glorify Christ as well as his Order of the Knights Templar could have been a plausible motive for two leaders imprisoned in this hypothetical scenario, but only that what they said during their last hours were God's truth in the eyes of their fellow colleagues in general. The martyrdom they proclaimed would have been in line with the courage and faith displayed by Jacques de Molay and Geoffroi de Charney in their last moments. Are we willing to question their motives and claim it was because the two Templars were able to commit suicide in order they could ensure that their corrupt Order, with its unconventional beliefs and practices would have the reputation of being sacked without just cause? The idea of deceit as Molay's motive for his death as a martyr will be in conflict with the facts we have about him - straight and trustworthy. These speculations are beyond the limits of historical evidence and common sense.

Was it likely it was possible that de Molay sincerely proclaimed the Order's innocence despite realizing that some bizarre actions actually existed (although not at the level described by the prosecution)? Strangely, yes. Being a Grand Master Jacques de Molay may have had access to information which was hidden from the other brothers (if there was any knowledge of this). In this case, he might believe, for example that the irregularities observed in Templar inductions were initially beneficial in evaluating prospective recruits. Additionally regardless the fact that de Molay understood the specifics however, he would certainly have understood that whatever the motivations for those practices, these were insignificant to Templars in their daily lives and their beliefs. Also, de Molay knew for his part that he and others were absolved from any sins they may have committed. He had reason to believe that no matter how many Templars were examined the majority of them would have were subject to papal absolution. Jacques de Molay was also conscious it was the case that the Order disbanded with no any official condemnation by the Church because of the absence of evidence. In short the situation, it was the Grand Master's instinct that his Order had been innocent and pure as a faithful group of Catholics who were orthodox Catholics.

Conclusion

In the span of two centuries, the Order of the Knights Templar was a key player in the political, military as well as the spiritual and economic life in Western Europe and the Levant. It is clear that the Order had the capacity to revitalize and reorganize its own organization following the destruction to its Holy Land. If it had been allowed to remain the negative consequences of its actions could have been more evident in the present world. Unfortunately, the demise of Knights Templar sends a negative message that dedication and effort could be "rewarded" by adversity and the libel. Therefore, it is crucial to seek justice in the past where current justice has failed to fulfill. We've observed that because of the absence of evidence tangible as well as the ineffective use of torture for confessing, the documents of Templar cases in France are not to be taken at for what they are in terms of finding the guilt or innocence and guilt of the Order. While the Chinon Parchment appears to is in line with the same pattern of mismanagement by the judiciary as documents that were produced by French inquisitors, it provides an alternative view of the trials. Due to the inability of interest to the full depositions and the general indifference to investigating possible themes and leads that were discussed in confessions by officials of the Order, it is possible to conclude that even within the top level of Pope's Curia doubts were raised regarding the admissibility of these confessions. Confessions and absoluteions, while appearing connected according to the words of the Chinon Parchment, in actuality had two distinct paths. If the prisoners agreed to re-record their testimony to a certain extent they could surely get an absolution from the Pope. In particular, Geoffroi de Gonneville was allowed to be pardoned without having to confess any thing that technically required pardon (unlike his earlier testimony before the papacy in Paris). The absolution was granted in the case of denouncing "the confessed and any other heresy" it can be stated that Knights Templar who appeared in the presence of papal commissions during 2013's summer had the chance to begin fresh as regards the spiritual status of their members was as it was. The well-known fact Jacques de Molay was able to regularly attend mass throughout the rest of his time shows his orthodoxy status according to the Church.

Chinon Parchment Chinon Parchment is an important document of the papal absolution granted to the most senior Templars. It is also important to consider it as a part of absolution granted to people who belong to the order, whose statements were taken up in the presence of the Pope and his commissioners between June and in early July in that same year. The fact is that the case of those who were Knights Templar was a legal matter, more be required to protect the Order from being destroyed. Clement V's weak dealings with King France as well as his uncertainty regarding the future significance in the military, rendered it difficult for him to stop trials even though there was no trust regarding the outcome they were generating.

The evidence that are from Knights Templar trials are voluminous and troubling. They include a lot of disturbing details, which are which could be damaging to the image that was earned by the Order. Understanding the context in the conditions under which these depositions were taken is essential. From my own experience, digging deeper into these documents and looking at the way they were covered in this book has brought me closer to understanding that the statements that Grandmaster Jacques de Molay about the order's purity and innocence can be believed after all.

It is possible to draw lessons drawn from the story that took place during the Knights Templar. One of the most important is that even though truth may be very fragile however, its shelf-life is a long time. It's been for a long time since anyone was able to gain or gain anything from what was known as the Templar trials. It is still a good feeling to know what really was going on with the most prestigious army of during the Middle Ages.

www.ingramcontent.com/pod-product-compliance
Lightning Source LLC
Chambersburg PA
CBHW050405120526
44590CB00015B/1830